Insider Guide

Negotiating Your Salary & Perks

2nd Edition

WetFeet ®
Helping you make smarter career decisions.

WetFeet, Inc.

The Folger Building
101 Howard Street, Suite 300
San Francisco, CA 94105
Phone: (415) 284-7900 or 1-800-926-4JOB
Fax: (415) 284-7910
Website: www.WetFeet.com

Negotiating Your Salary & Perks

By Duncan Haberly & Robert A. Fish
ISBN: 1-58207-428-3

Table of Contents

Negotiating Your Salary and Perks at a Glance

Before You Interview

- Building your bargaining power is a critical goal of all of your interactions with the employer, from your initial introduction (whether via referral or resume submission) to your final interview. The bargaining power you manage to accrue will play a major role in your compensation negotiations.

- The best preparation you can do for a salary negotiation is to benchmark compensation for the career, company, industry, and region you are interviewing for.

- The earlier you enter the interview process the better. If you manage to get your foot in the door while the employer is still defining the job parameters, you have a better chance of contributing to the job description and then of being selected for the position.

- Before you can enter into a successful negotiation of any sort, you need to establish your priorities, so you can decide where to draw your line in the sand.

Negotiate the Interview Process

Strategic negotiation fundamentals:

1. Self-knowledge

2. Effective presentation

3. Increasing the value of the job

4. Increasing the value of you in the job

Tips for interviewing like a negotiator:

- Connect with the decision-maker.

- Be enthusiastic and connect personally.

- Don't ask for no as an answer.

- Explore all that the employer can offer.

- Benchmark the compensation and the position for the company, industry, and region.

- Discuss your salary history intelligently.

- Don't be the first to name a salary.

- Continue to interview elsewhere.

What's Negotiable?

- Understand the objective constraints for the position you're interviewing for. Knowing these will help you focus your negotiation on those items that are truly negotiable.

- Your negotiation should begin with the job responsibilities, not with compensation. After all, if you can negotiate increased responsibility, you're much more likely to win a negotiation for increased compensation, too!

- To structure an effective negotiation, you'll need to know what your goals are and what your requirements are—in other words, what do you need to survive?

The Negotiation

The fundamentals:

- Always negotiate with the decision-maker

- Ask probing questions

- Get comfortable and keep it simple

- Create win-win situations

- Pick your battles to win the war

Potential responses:

- Based on benchmarking and research
- Based on your own needs
- Based on the employer's needs
- Based on finding creative alternatives
- Designed to create tension
- Designed to reduce tension

The employer's bag of tricks:

- Imaginary competitors
- Delays
- Rushing your decision
- Empty promises
- Financial hardship

The Decision

When the negotiation concludes, it's time for a few final steps:

- Be sure to get the final offer in writing so there's no confusion later.
- If you have competing offers, you'll want to consult your decision matrix.
- Finally, it's time to decline graciously, delay your decision, or accept enthusiastically!

Before You Interview

- Overview

- Strategy vs. Tactics

- Bargaining Power

- Know the Market: Benchmark!

- Timing: The Early Bird and All That

- Establish Your Priorities

- A Firm Negotiation Wins Respect

Overview

You've jumped through all the hoops. You've developed a great resume, identified a promising job opportunity, performed well in rounds of interviews, and now the call has finally come: They want you. Congratulations!

But wait—the most challenging part of your job search has arrived: It's time to negotiate your compensation and working conditions.

A negotiation is a competition between parties for resources and benefits. A compensation negotiation is just like any other negotiation in the business world, with one glaring difference: *Your* resources and benefits are on the table. Even if you have the most aggressive and risk-seeking personality, it is common in a job negotiation to suddenly find yourself feeling timid and risk-averse because the stakes on the table are your happiness and security. If you're in a strong position—lots of offers, outstanding technical skills, little competition—negotiating may be a matter of naming your price. Even so, strategy is important. You want your manager and coworkers to be glad to have you, not resentful of your demands.

Besides, few of us are this fortunate. The typical candidate really wants the job, is terrified of losing it by being too aggressive, and doesn't negotiate effectively—if at all. This Insider Guide aims to replace that fear with confidence, giving you the tools to take ownership of the negotiation process at every step and feel secure that you have maximized the resources and benefits available to you. We will show you how to improve your standing with the employer, equip you with tools to assess your position and determine negotiating priorities, discuss a range of potential negotiating points, demonstrate how to handle a variety of situations, and prepare you to field the tough questions.

Whether this is your first job offer or your tenth, you'll do yourself a favor by honing your negotiation skills. Whatever the firm's initial offer is, it can often be improved—in many cases dramatically—through savvy negotiating. And once you're on the job, it'll be difficult to get the same boost, even with stellar performance.

The negotiation process begins much earlier than you may realize—in fact, it begins with the employer's first notice of you, whether it's your resume, the referral you received from a former colleague, or your first interview. It is therefore imperative that you build a strong starting position. Your confidence, the way you present yourself, and how you discuss the job are all part of your negotiations. If you've become the clear top candidate for a position, you obviously have more bargaining power than if you appear little better than the next-best candidate. By the time you get to the bargaining table, a lot of your negotiating has already been accomplished—for better or worse.

Already at that point? Don't worry. We'll show you how to assess your bargaining position—whatever it is—and use solid negotiating tactics to get the best possible offer. Maybe you can improve your salary by 5 percent, or even 20 percent. Maybe you can negotiate an early review with a raise for strong performance. And then there are bonuses, increased commission, stock options, educational benefits, extra vacation days, a flexible work schedule, a respected title, and increased challenges and responsibilities. These and a host of other factors could mean the difference between job satisfaction and early discontent.

The Bottom Line

Your time is one of your most valuable possessions. And when you take a job, you are giving up most of your waking hours to help others achieve their objectives. Isn't it worth investing a little time up front to make sure you're compensated at your full value?

Practice the techniques described in this Insider Guide, do the research to back up your requests, and you can negotiate an excellent compensation package—not just a good salary, but your other must-haves as well, and even a few nice-to-have items. If you do this well, your employer will also be pleased with the agreement—and even more impressed with you. Note that the principles here also apply to negotiating a raise, winning a coveted job assignment, reaching agreements with coworkers, and many other negotiations on and off the job.

Strategy vs. Tactics

A successful negotiation requires both good strategic preparation and tactical execution. Optimally, your preparation for your compensation negotiation begins before you secure your first interview. Strategy is the foundation—what you do to ensure that your bargaining position is as strong as it can be—and you should start working on it before you sit down to hammer out details with your future employer.

A well-thought-out negotiation strategy makes the most of your talents, education, job experiences, and recommendations, while neutralizing your limitations. In short, your strategy builds your bargaining power to its maximum potential before you walk into the actual negotiation.

Tactics are your actions at the negotiation table to achieve the best outcome considering the strength of your bargaining power. The first three chapters of this Insider Guide will help you develop your negotiation strategy and build your bargaining power. The fifth chapter, "The Negotiation," is your guide to using the right negotiation tactics to capitalize on your bargaining power and stay ahead of the other side of the table.

Bargaining Power

Bargaining power is what you have if there's an oil field on fire and you're the only outfit able to be on the scene smothering the flames tomorrow. Bargaining power is what you have if you are far and away the top salesperson at the leading company in a very competitive industry. Bargaining power is what you have when a company's database is hacked via the Internet and you are the only engineer in the industry who specializes in recovery after that kind of attack. With this kind of bargaining power, it doesn't make much difference what your peers are charging. You can name your price because you have a skill set and background that employers believe they have to have.

If you can transform yourself from just another qualified candidate into *the* candidate, you won't have much need for fancy negotiating tactics when it comes time to agree on terms—your increased bargaining power will move mountains. Get yourself into this position, and you can expect to upgrade your job title. The company may entrust you with a wider range of responsibilities—which means richer experiences and more opportunities. You may be able to report to a higher-level supervisor and have greater decision-making power. All this translates to a higher salary, access to more privileges, and speedier career development.

If, on the other hand, the employer sees you as no more qualified or desirable than many of the other candidates, your bargaining power will suffer and your efforts to significantly improve a job offer will almost certainly inspire a second look at your competitors. Making the company feel that it *needs* you specifically will get you a better deal than deploying every negotiating trick in the book (this book or any other) from a position of weakness.

Put plainly, bargaining power is the sum of all the impressions you've made on an employer. A referral from a respected source is a great first deposit in your bargaining-power bank. More than one adds to your account. An excellent resume and enthusiastic references contribute still more.

An impressive first interview, in which you articulate your strengths, show that you know what it takes to do the job, and share some insights based on your own research, can be a big boost to your bargaining power. If your follow-up to that first meeting demonstrates more work on your part and real insights into the business, you'll get a second interview and still more bargaining power.

When your meetings with your potential coworkers go well, you raise your bargaining power again. Perhaps you offer to tackle a short-term assignment (for pay, if there is substantial work involved) and show off your talents; now your bargaining power is through the roof—they really want you! By the time you are in what's generally recognized as the negotiation process, you're dealing from a position of maximum strength.

Know the Market: Benchmark!

One of the key principles of strategic negotiation is to know the market. For maximum leverage, you need to answer the following questions:

1. What is the going rate for the position? (This will probably require some research—likely sources include industry trade magazines, websites, and Sibson and Mercer or other salary surveys used by human resources departments.)

2. What positives or negatives apply—to you or the job—that might justify a deviation from the going rate?

In this Insider Guide, we will return time and again to the importance of research and benchmarking. Benchmarking is the identification and comparison of market and competitor standards and valuations for a negotiation term. Put simply for our purposes here, benchmarking is figuring out how much other companies are paying for your skill set and the type of job you are trying to get.

Take it from us, specific knowledge of how the market values the things you are negotiating for is the single greatest asset that you can take into a compensation negotiation. No amount of smooth talking and negotiation tricks can beat a fully prepared negotiator who has taken the time to identify and research the values associated with her skill set, the position, the company, and the industry (particularly if she has gone so far as to collect competing offers).

Benchmarking works because externally validated and relevant information neutralizes the employer's bargaining power and helps reset the hiring manager's expectations to a range closer to your asking terms—effectively boxing him in.

Finally, having solid benchmarking data makes you comfortable in your negotiating position and your demands—freeing you up to focus on the details of your negotiation technique once you are in the room.

See the "For Your Reference" chapter at the end of this Insider Guide to find resources you can use to help you benchmark salary ranges.

Timing: The Early Bird and All That

A company rarely decides to seek a new employee on the spur of the moment. Unless it's simply a matter of replacing an employee who's moved on, such decisions typically follow a three-stage process:

1. A problem or need is identified. There's too much work to be done by the existing staff, a problem with quality or customer satisfaction, or a need to develop new business.

2. Solutions are considered. Should several employees' jobs be redefined so that their talents are put to better use? Should an existing staff member be moved to a new position? (If so, that person's old position will have to be filled.) Should a new employee be hired to fill the position? Or should most of the work be outsourced?

3. The job is defined. The company decides to create a new position. The next questions to be answered: Where will the money come from? Who will the person report to? What will the job description include?

Only after all three stages are completed does the company go to the market—advertise the position, post it on the Internet, hire a recruiter to find the right person. If you enter the game at this point, you're likely to face a fair amount of competition, which means diminished bargaining power. If you can enter at an earlier stage, you gain several advantages:

- You can influence how the company sees its needs and how best to address them. This is an opportunity to tailor the job description to fit your qualifications and make full use of your talents. It's also a chance to boost the job to the highest level possible—and more responsibility equals more money.

- You allow the company to solve the problem quickly, avoiding the time and expense of working through all three stages, not to mention sorting through reams of resumes.

- Because at this point there are few—or no—other candidates, the company is less likely to base its compensation offer on what similarly qualified candidates might cost. And even if you can't get the salary as high as you'd like, you'll be in a prime position to win other forms of compensation and benefits.

Getting considered early usually means entering the discussions informally. If your first contact with the company is an informational meeting (perhaps set up through one of your networking contacts), you can talk about your background and interests without the pressure of an interview situation, get feedback on any research you've done, and learn about the industry and the business from an insider.

In the process, you may see a need or problem at the company that has not yet been defined (entering at stage 1) or find out about one whose solution has not yet been settled (entering at stage 2). You'll be able to follow up on the information meeting with a letter or e-mail describing the additional thinking or research you've done (based on the insider perspective you've gained), which sets you up for another meeting. Once you're in the discussion loop and have established your credibility, you're in a well primed to land a position that's tailored for you. (WetFeet's *Networking Works!* offers step-by-step advice for networking effectively to increase your career opportunities.)

Finally, keep in mind that taking on a short-term project can dramatically improve your bargaining power. While you're holding informal discussions about the company's needs, you're in an excellent position to suggest that you take on a short-term project addressing a critical issue. (This is also a great way to make yourself stand out if you've entered the hiring process after stage 3.) Possible projects include the following:

- Conducting a customer survey
- Organizing and running a focus group
- Evaluating a proposed employee-benefit program
- Exploring and reporting on better sources for contract manufacturing
- Flow-charting operating procedures and designing a new workflow
- Investigating the willingness of another organization (a complementary business or a nonprofit agency) to enter into an alliance
- Identifying new business or sales prospects
- Analyzing expense-reduction opportunities
- Developing a software solution

Properly structured, such a project gives you several potential advantages:

- You can demonstrate the quality of your work, rather than relying solely on your resume and the inferences people make when interviewing you.

- You get to operate on the inside, where you'll get a full picture of the firm's needs. This kind of knowledge will prove valuable later when you're discussing the job and what you bring to it.

- You can charge a daily rate that may be substantially more than what you'd earn doing similar work as a full-time employee. So when the company does offer to bring you aboard, your frame of reference on salary—and theirs— is this daily rate, rather than the lower rate that might otherwise apply. For example, a short-term project rate of $450 a day translates, at 250 working days per year, to an annual salary of $112,500. All right, you may agree to a bargain rate of $95,000, considering that they're offering you a benefits package. Still, this is much better than the $70,000 you had previously hoped to get! (Your daily rate depends on the nature of the assignment. If you're filling in for someone and need considerable supervision, the rate could reasonably be from 100 to 150 percent of that person's salary prorated by the day. [Go ahead and ask if you don't know what the person's salary is.] But if you're working on a high-priority project, adding your own expertise to the manager's, or improving business opportunities, for example, your rate can be considerably higher—as much as double a staff person's regular pay.)

Note: It's essential that any demonstration project show you in your best light—that you meet the deadline, produce more than you promise, and provide facts and insights that are clearly worth having. Spend whatever time it takes to make sure this is the outcome. Don't take on a short-term project if you are not sure you can do an impressive job—shoddy work will make you a far less attractive candidate than if you'd done nothing at all. A safe rule-of-thumb is that you should only take on a short-term project if you have direct previous experience performing that kind of work and are fully comfortable with your skill set in that area.

Establish Your Priorities

Consider what things really matter to you in your next job. Salary could be paramount, or perhaps the credibility that comes from working for a Fortune 50 company is the boost your career is craving, or reasonable hours and lots of vacation time might matter most because you have young children. You will discover as you go through this exercise that some of the things that matter most to you are not negotiable (e.g., the company's Fortune 50 status), and others are prime negotiation targets (e.g., vacation time).

Know what really matters to you: List the highest priority factors that will contribute most to your job satisfaction, then assign each a relative weight out of a total of 100 percent happiness. For example:

Career opportunity = 30 percent (of your happiness in a given job)
Salary = 30 percent
Rapport with supervisor = 20 percent
Benefits = 10 percent
Location = 10 percent

Keep these priorities in mind as you interview and solicit offers. They will plug into your decision-making later on and help determine (1) whether an offer passes muster and, if so, (2) how it compares to your other options.

A Firm Negotiation
Wins Respect

Keep the following in mind while interviewing and negotiating: A good manager will be impressed by an employee who handles himself well in a negotiation. A good manager knows that healthy negotiation skills demonstrate a maturity and depth of business sensibility that will benefit the company once you are on board—even if you will not be working in a position traditionally given negotiation responsibilities. A job candidate who ably protects his own interests during the hiring process is more likely to become an employee who competently represents his employer's interests.

This is not to say that you won't encounter hiring managers who try to bully or cajole you and appear put out by your firm approach, but as long as you remain ethical and follow the strategies and tactics outlined here without stooping to the personal or petty, you should find that your new manager respects your strength of will and purpose.

Negotiate the
Interview Process

- Strategic Negotiation Fundamentals

- Tips for Interviewing Like a Negotiator

Strategic Negotiation Fundamentals

Strategic negotiation aims for more than simply landing the job—it's the conscious process of creating conditions that will give you that job on the best possible terms. You're working toward three objectives simultaneously:

1. Improving your chances of getting the job offer

2. Increasing the value the employer places on the position

3. Creating the perception that you are the person for the job

Think of your strategy as being built on four cornerstones, each of which will lift you to a higher and more solid starting point than you would otherwise have for discussions on salary and benefits. Let's examine them one at a time.

1. Self-Knowledge

How can you expect a potential employer to understand your strengths, goals, and working style if you're not clear about them yourself?

Your resume is but a brief summary of who you are and what you are capable of. Take the trouble to list some of your proudest accomplishments, then write a short "story" about each of them, following a situation-action-result pattern. Try to find common threads in these stories that reflect your major strengths. These might be creative problem-solving, skill at organizing facts, the ability to listen well and find a consensus, talent for motivating others, thinking well under pressure, or whatever. These become the main theme of your presentation: what you've accomplished, how you accomplished it, and how you can put these strengths to work in a new position.

Think about your work habits as well. Do you work best in a high-pressure atmosphere or one that's more relaxed? Do you like to work alone or as part of a group? Or do you prefer a combination of the two? Do you like a lot of socializing or prefer to be more private? These factors will affect your happiness and performance at a new job, so you should consider them when making a job decision.

Ask other people about their impressions of you, particularly people you plan to use as references. Their responses will help you select what to emphasize in the messages you convey about yourself. Once you have developed the perspective, don't be afraid to tell your references what you plan to emphasize about yourself in interviews. This can be an effective way of ensuring that your references stay "on message."

2. Effective Presentation

Develop a 2-minute presentation about yourself, and use it whenever possible. Devote about 30 seconds to your career, your educational background, and your key strengths; 60 seconds to describing two key accomplishments that illustrate those strengths (the stories will come in handy here); and the final 30 seconds to the kind of work and responsibilities you're seeking. Don't let yourself go over 2½ minutes, lest you sound too self-centered, or under 1½ minutes, lest you seem like a lightweight. Practice delivering this presentation, not as a word-for-word recital, but extemporaneously, based on the key points you want to make. (You'll find more in-depth instructions on constructing and delivering such presentations in WetFeet's *Job Hunting A to Z: Landing the Job You Want.*)

Use this 2-minute presentation at the beginning of every information meeting and first interview. It will give you immediate credibility and answer most of the interviewer's questions about your background and goals, leaving you free to ask questions about the company and the job. Be prepared with great questions, and you'll enhance the first impression.

 Spin the Negatives

A savvy interviewer or negotiator may try to destabilize your presentation (or subsequent negotiation position) by tying your hiring chances, compensation, title, or responsibilities to something negative in your work history. If you have had some rough patches in your career, or you have had a manager who did not appreciate your style, it is imperative that you own these negatives and turn a question about them into an opportunity to either deflect to a positive story or demonstrate how you overcame those issues.

Here are some examples of negatives and how to deal with them when brought up in an interview or negotiation:

You were laid off from a previous job.

There is no shame in being laid off; in fact, it happens to almost everyone at one time or another. Come up with a breezy two-sentence explanation for the company's layoffs, and then finish with an upbeat recitation of the opportunities that the layoff presented. For example, you were able to finish school, you toured Europe, you learned some woodworking, and—best of all—you were freed up to look for more meaningful work at a great company like the employer's.

The trick here is to have a quick gloss for the layoff and then segue directly into a positive wrap-up that conveys equanimity and readiness to take on the next challenge. Also, avoid being cheesy, but don't underestimate a hiring manager's desire to hear genuine enthusiasm about the new position and the prospective employer.

Spin the Negatives (cont'd)

You were fired from a previous job.

This one is a bit tougher, but you absolutely should have a packaged explanation at the ready when the subject comes up—because it's likely that it will. The best explanation openly acknowledges that the situation wasn't optimal and looks for a way to tell the story with a positive ending. Above all, you do not want to get bogged down in a long-winded explanation of how you weren't wrong in the first place or how other folks had it in for you. Even if you were arguably in the right, most hiring managers don't want to hear the whole story—and, given the details, will likely tend to sympathize with your former manager.

Instead, describe the problem in three to four short dispassionate sentences and then speak about what you have done in the interim to fix your contribution to the problem. If you were fired for poor attitude, you might talk about how you started volunteering and realized how much you previously took for granted. If you were fired for being constantly late, you might talk about how you saw a sleep special-ist and now sleep 8 hours a night. Most important, don't lie about either the prob-lem or the solution; a prospective employer may check your story and blackball you in the industry or profession if the story doesn't bear out.

You quit your last job.

Assuming you didn't leave your former employer without notice, there is absolutely no shame to this. Characterize the decision as one you made, after careful consid-eration, to give you the time and focus to find a better opportunity at a great com-pany like the employer's.

If you did quit your last job without notice and for a thinly justified reason—and you know there is potential animosity remaining at your former employer, we suggest employing an approach similar to that given above for explaining a firing. Emphasize what has happened in the interim to develop your maturity.

3. Increasing the Value of the Job

Often a position that seems mundane is actually vitally important to the business. Performing it well can bring in extra revenue or stop major losses. Doing mediocre work can be costly. Your first questions should draw the interviewer out about the nature of the job—and highlight the substantive connections the job has to the department and company's success. For example:

Employer: We are a fairly young company, but, as you can tell from the job posting, this is a standard account manager position, with the typical sales support functions and tools that you find anywhere in the insurance industry. In this job, you would be tasked with supporting the accounts of ten outside salespeople who are based out on the East Coast and pretty much constantly out on the road selling to clients.

Candidate: Great! Could you tell me how, and how often, those salespeople update their client contact and sales databases while on the road?

The candidate knows from research/experience that sales database support is a common problem.

Employer: Well, they are supposed to do so before noon every day, via the Internet, but you will often find that they can't get a stable modem connection from the road. When this happens, they may call you directly before the office opens here on the West Coast and ask you to update their accounts manually and then check to make sure that they have the proper client list and tasking for the afternoon's sales calls.

Candidate: And do these updates feed into any other systems?

This is a great question because it prompts the hiring manager to describe how this part of the job affects the rest of the department—and even the rest of the company.

Employer: Absolutely! The company's rolling financial projections are fed by the sales department's database. Oh, and the daily sales updates also feed into the marketing department's automated overnight mailings of sales brochures, offering targeted upgrade and cross-sell opportunities to customers while they still have the previous day's sales calls fresh in their minds.

Candidate: So, as I understand the position, my responsibilities include (1) keeping existing customer accounts happy; (2) making myself available to my salespeople *whenever* they need assistance to complete and report a sale; (3) helping ensure that the finance department is getting the complete and current sales data it needs to optimally project revenues; and (4) making sure that my salespeople's target lists for direct mailings are passed to the marketing department in a timely manner, so that maximum sales-per-account are achieved. That is an exciting range of important responsibilities!

Your next goal is to make sure the interviewer recognizes the job's full value—particularly any currently unrealized value. You can do this by identifying a challenge the position presents and then taking the interviewer through a series of leading questions to evaluate the challenge and raise the perceived value of solving it. The two sample dialogues that follow illustrate this value-increasing process.

Business Development Example

Candidate: This position is in the business development department. Could you tell me how your business development department integrates with your sales department?

Employer: The business development team identifies and negotiates strategic partnerships and our sales team identifies and prosecutes sales targets for our products.

Candidate: And do your partnership deals ever include sales of your products to new partners?

Employer: Well, probably not as often as our CEO and CFO would like.

Candidate: Why do you think that is the case?

Employer: While they are great negotiators and analysts, our business development team members come primarily out of strategy consulting and legal practice and tend to focus on the strategic and legel elements of deals, and not the near-term sales possibilities.

Candidate: That's interesting. I talked to your team members and studied some of your partnerships and it looks to me like there is the possibility to sell the company's products in at least one-third of your strategic deals. My estimate is that an additional $1 million per year in sales is possible through your strategic deals.

Employer: I am not sure that kind of sales revenue is possible in business development, but I would love to hear more about how you think you could achieve those numbers in this position.

Candidate: Absolutely. I have worked in both sales and business development and can show you how to integrate sales transactions into as many business development deals as possible.

Employer: That sounds great. I can tell you that senior management would be very excited to hear about additional revenue that wouldn't require a new line of business or marketing spending.

Candidate: Excellent, and while we look at my sales estimates, let's also talk about an additional commission structure on sales revenue so that I am always motivated to keep an eye out for the immediate sales opportunities inside broader strategic deals.

Inventory-Management Example

Candidate: From our discussion last time, I understand the position you have in mind for me is in inventory management. Could you tell more about your needs in that area?

Actually, the candidate has spent the time since the last meeting learning all she could about the subject.

Employer: Yes. We need someone to keep track of our daily incoming shipments, our daily outgoing shipments, and our inventory levels.

Candidate: Are you experiencing a problem now—revenues not in synch with other numbers, or other discrepancies?

An on-target question based on thinking about what inventory management involves.

Employer: Unfortunately, yes. We have a shrinkage rate of about 2 percent, which is way too high. And too many damaged goods, which costs us plenty.

Candidate: You told me earlier that monthly sales are about $600,000, so if I'm right, you're losing $12,000 a month in shrinkage. And about how much would you say the damaged-goods problem is causing?

Employer: At least that much—maybe more.

Candidate: If you had a system for relating orders to shipments, outbound quality assurance, and damage accountability, would that help you with your customers relations, too?

A shrewd question, based on an article the candidate read in Industry Week *about a company's new inventory management system.*

Employer: Definitely. Too often the wrong materials go to a job site, or some have to be returned, and it takes time and patience to get it straightened out.

Candidate: And there's the risk that the customer will go elsewhere in the future, right? What would it cost you to replace a major account?

This demonstrates the candidate's ability to relate improved practices to tangible value.

Employer: A lot. It's taken years to build up our 15 major accounts.

Candidate: If I can develop a system that reduces shrinkage to a negligible level and eliminates shipment errors by 75 percent or more, would that be pretty valuable to you?

Audacious, but she isn't saying she can do it alone, or in a month.

Employer: Definitely! I'd be happy to get you a bonus if you could do that.

Candidate: I've met some big challenges before, but I'll need your cooperation to do this. And I'd be glad to discuss a bonus, but I'll also need a higher base salary than what you mentioned.

Employer: Well—let's talk about it. What do you have in mind?

The candidate seems to think quickly here, which creates more credibility. But, if this is your second meeting with the manager, you've had the time to do some thinking, research, and planning, and to come up with questions that lead the discussion where you want it to go.

In both of these scenarios, the job seeker guides the discussion by asking questions. She may have already known or have been able to guess the answers to some of these questions, but when she has the interviewer state the case for her, she strengthens the interviewer's commitment to that interpretation.

Also note that, in both situations, the questions follow a sequence. First are questions that characterize the situation: Business development isn't driving enough sales; inventories are out of control. Next come questions that elicit the reasons for the situation: The current staff isn't sales-oriented; there is no set system for ensuring that shipments match orders. The questions that follow are designed to increase the perceived urgency or importance of solving the problem: Hundreds of thousands of sales dollars are being left on the table;

the company may lose customers to another vendor. The final questions confirm the value of a solution to the employer: easy additional revenue; satisfied, loyal customers.

Using this approach, you can nudge future employers into increasing—in their minds and even in their own words—the value of the position.

It takes some practice to develop leading questions well and use them skillfully. As with other negotiating strategies and tactics, we suggest you perfect your technique in situations with less at stake than a job negotiation—renting an apartment, say, or negotiating group rates for a weekend trip with friends. You might also practice this technique by rehearsing with a friend or family member. And don't be afraid to turn to well-positioned friends or family members for help in developing these kinds of questions.

4. Increasing the Value of *You* in the Job

It's not enough that the hiring manager realizes the value of the job. She must also believe that you are the best person to do the job. You have a big head start, of course, if you've created a sense of urgency about filling the position and gained acknowledgment of its current and potential value. You now seem insightful and knowledgeable about the position you are interviewing for.

But performance is still paramount in the employer's mind. The employer's chief concerns are as follows:

- Will you meet performance expectations?
- Will you meet deadlines?
- Will you be challenged and interested in this position?
- Will you stay committed or hit the road the minute a slightly better offer comes along?
- Will you fit in well with the company's culture, needs, and expectations?

To address these concerns, you first need to ask yourself some questions—and answer them honestly. Is this a job you care about enough to do what it takes to meet expectations? If you do meet expectations, will the money, recognition, or intrinsic value of the work be rewarding enough to you? Can the expectations be met? If you think the manager's expectations are unrealistic, but the job appeals to you otherwise, try listing the main responsibilities as you understand them and breaking each one down into its component parts. Tell the manager you want to review the list and make sure you're correctly estimating the time needed to do the job at the level expected. The manager may classify some duties as less important or point out where help is available. You can then add up the time needed for each task, plus meetings and administrative work, and get a clear idea about whether the job can be done in the hours you're willing to devote to it.

Think about whether you'll be happy in the job 6 months from now. Will there be enough challenges and learning opportunities to keep the job fresh over time? Is solving the initial problem what intrigues you, rather than the ongoing responsibilities? Now is the time to recognize the situation for what it is. Do you commonly fall prey to the grass-is-always-greener syndrome, or do you usually stick with what you start? If you tend to jump from task to task, maybe consulting or a start-up would suit you better than a more structured environment. Only when you are clear on your preferences and feelings about the job can you make the kind of compelling, from-the-heart pitch that is likely to win over an astute manager.

To answer the "Can you do it?" question, the employer usually considers your resume, your responses to interview questions, and your references, and compares all candidates in those areas. Asking smart, probing questions during interviews and demonstrating that you understand the business, the position, its challenges, and how you could add value in creative and efficient ways will help the employer recognize the additional benefits of having *you* in the job. Tying the challenges of the position to solutions you have successfully implemented in past positions increases your attractiveness. Establishing friendly connections with your prospective coworkers also helps propel you ahead of the pack.

But you can do even more to distinguish yourself:

> One option is a testimonial letter describing how you solved a problem or came through in a crisis. For maximum credibility, the letter should be addressed to you, not "to whom it may concern," and phrased as an expression of appreciation for a job well done. If you don't have a letter like this on hand, you can ask one of your references to write one—you might even get faster results by providing a draft.

> You may be able to demonstrate your abilities by taking on a short-term project, or auditioning by briefly performing some aspect of the job— customer service, teaching, programming, or selling, for example.

> Finally, consider the homily, "Actions speak louder than words." When the employer is on the verge of making an offer, but you haven't yet discussed pay and benefits, look for a way to make an investment in the job. You could give the employer a list of things you'd try to achieve in the first 30 days, noting the actions you'd take to meet these goals. Maybe you could accomplish a few of these beforehand. If so, they will serve as handy illustrations of your willingness to do this job when you sit down to discuss pay and benefits.

Now that you've added substantially to your perceived value and bargaining power, you should be a top candidate.

Tips for Interviewing Like a Negotiator

Connect with the Decision-Maker

As you learn more about the job opportunity, you will want to identify the decision-maker on the hire, typically a manager in the department in which you will be working, but sometimes a recruiter or even a human resources (HR) department manager or associate. Often, you may initially deal with an assistant to the HR manager or decision-maker. You will need to impress these intermediaries to get to the final decision-maker, but you should understand that they may not be responsible for making the hiring decision and negotiating an offer.

When you do get to the decision-maker, ask probing questions about their most pressing needs and catalog the answers. Later in the negotiation, if you can meet some or all of those needs, the manager can probably meet more of your needs.

And, whatever the structure of the interview process, make sure that you negotiate your package with the decision-maker, *not* an intermediary. The decision-maker has a far better understanding of the job than an intermediary like an HR manager. The decision-maker also has a greater sense of urgency about filling the position and more flexibility in addressing your needs. Besides, this is the person you'll be working with—you want to make sure you reach a mutually satisfying agreement.

Finally, identifying and getting in front of the decision-maker before your competitors makes you the benchmark by which the subsequent candidates will be judged—which can help you short-circuit their chances of ever being seen by the decision-maker. Don't be a pest, but take any reasonable opportunity to introduce yourself and your resume to the decision-maker; always have extra copies of your resume and cover letter with you when you are interviewing.

Be Enthusiastic and Connect Personally

As you likely know from experience—and from reading the WetFeet Insider Guide to interviewing, *Ace Your Interview!*—a positive attitude and the willingness to make a personal connection when interviewing go a long, long way toward getting hiring managers and prospective co-workers excited about choosing you over your competitors.

And the same enthusiasm that gets you noticed as a candidate should also serve as a major step in your negotiation strategy; it is a truism that an enthusiastic applicant is one that a hiring manager is generally going to feel more comfortable negotiating an offer with. Once you have received the offer, you will be able to capitalize on the comfort and ease that you have engendered during the interview process to disarm the other side at key negotiation moments and to, most importantly, maximize your final offer.

To illustrate this point, let's look at a couple of behavioral options for interviewing: Abel is a candidate interviewing at Credible, Inc., with hiring manager, Baker.

Scenario 1

Abel, not wanting to waste Baker's time, introduces himself pleasantly—but without a lot of chit-chat—and immediately turns to his value-increasing strategies and asking questions specifically about the position and hiring terms.

Scenario 2

Abel introduces himself and starts by asking some very positive and general questions of Baker, looking for an opportunity to express enthusiasm about things that are important to Baker (e.g., Baker's children's photos, college alma mater, hometown, hobbies) and complimenting Baker's team, his management philosophy, the company, and the company's products. Where appropriate, Abel mentions personal connections to what he learns from Baker (e.g., a shared hometown, alma mater, hobby). Abel then moves to his value-increasing strategies and asking questions about the position and hiring terms—all the while continuing to make personal connections to Baker whenever possible.

You might correctly guess that Baker is likely to feel more positively toward Abel in the second scenario. This personal goodwill connects Abel to Baker in a way that puts the coming negotiation on a different footing than in the first scenario. To the degree that Abel was enthusiastic and managed to form a personal connection, Baker may feel a duty to treat Abel more like a friend or respected colleague than just another interviewee off the street—meaning that Baker may automatically adjust the initial offer to Abel's benefit and then subsequently negotiate it with less aggressive back-and-forth.

A corollary to that last benefit often goes underappreciated: your ability to push harder and longer on the terms that you are trying to secure can often be directly proportional to the store of positive impressions and goodwill you have accumulated in your interactions before the negotiation started in earnest.

HR and hiring managers, as well as prospective co-workers, want to see enthusiasm and sense a comfortable fit. A qualified candidate who seems to think the world of the company and the position, and who makes an obvious effort to connect personally with everyone they meet, is more likely to get the offer—and then negotiate a better final offer—than a similarly situated candidate who doesn't express the same kind of enthusiasm. Don't be afraid to express your real enthusiasm for the job and, just as importantly, don't pass up a chance to connect personally with the interviewing staff. Once you have formed a positive impression and connected personally, you can play off this personal capital to negotiate your offer more aggressively than otherwise possible.

Remember: Your resume and skill set get you in the door, but genuine enthusiasm and the ability to connect personally are what often get you the offer and increase the hiring manager's willingness to meet your hiring terms during negotiations.

Don't Ask for No as an Answer

You may have noticed that good salespeople like to ask yes/no questions that are phrased so that the expected answer is yes. You can make use of this sales technique when interviewing and negotiating to avoid closing down the discussion with a question that begs a negative response. For example:

Wrong: So, you haven't considered creating cross-sell opportunities?

Right: Wouldn't the creation of cross-sell opportunities help your sales numbers?

Wrong: Is there any chance that you could go higher than $50,000?

Right: Wouldn't you agree that it is important for the company to stay competitive with other companies in this industry?

You would then highlight your favorable salary benchmarking data showing that the job normally commands $55,000.

Remember, this technique is useful when you need to gently lead the other side to a specific point you want to make. Work it in where you need to get around a probable "no" on an important negotiation item, but do not use it too repetitively or patronizingly; it can get old very quickly.

Explore All That the Employer Can Offer

A new job can have many features that you value, both financial and nonfinancial. The forms of financial compensation are many. Some of the following confer other benefits, but they all boil down to money:

- Salary (usually the base for figuring bonuses and raises)
- Signing bonus (often given if you are being induced to leave a good job)
- Moving allowance
- Housing allowance
- Bonuses (best if tied to measurable criteria)
- Early review for salary increase or promotion
- Commissions
- Health and other types of insurance
- Tuition reimbursement
- Stock awards or options
- 401(k) plan
- Severance package
- Club memberships, event tickets, food

Learn as much as you can about industry and company standards for each form of compensation before you sit down to negotiate. You'll find advice on when and how to negotiate for these and other items in "What's Negotiable?"

Financial compensation usually isn't the only consideration when evaluating a job offer. Other factors and forms of consideration that may be important to you include the following:

- Title
- Responsibilities
- The quality of the learning opportunity

- Rapport with your supervisor

- Respect for your colleagues

- The workplace atmosphere, whether intense or relaxed, competitive or mutually supportive, chaotic or organized

- Travel

- Recognition, speaking opportunities, media exposure

- The company's prestige

- The importance or value of what the organization produces

- Career-advancement opportunities

- Vacation and time-off policies

- Flexibility of the work schedule

- Location

- Commuting distance and related considerations (availability of public transportation or parking)

- On-site facilities, such as fitness and child-care centers

Benchmark, Benchmark, Benchmark

Benchmarking (i.e., researching and comparing) the broader job market's standards for compensation, title, responsibilities, and perks, based on the position, your skill set, and qualifications, will help you advance your case. For example, if you know what other companies are offering—or what other employees at the same company are receiving—you can use this information if the hiring manager seems to be giving you a lowball offer. You can express tactful surprise at the proposed salary and have the figures to back up your reaction. Without question, benchmarking is the single most important investment in your job negotiation that you can make. We have included it in this section because, as you interview, you should be taking what you learn about the position, the company, the industry, and then aggressively benchmarking those factors, along

The Interview Process

with your skill set and qualifications, against the market to help you properly set your asking terms and then support your negotiation positions.

How you benchmark is just as important as benchmarking itself. First, collect all data relevant to your situation; don't ignore data that contradicts your position. Once you have a solid range of data, you will want to figure out how to choose and present the specific data that best supports your position—without engaging in unethical or fraudulent behavior that could get you caught in a mischaracterization or—even worse—kicked out the door immediately. To be safe, always be clear with hiring managers about where you got a piece of data and do not mix data from different sources without highlighting each shift in source. And be prepared to defend your choices of some data over others.

Let's look at some examples of how to handle benchmarked data:

Your research into health benefits offered at the employer's competitors reveals that Competitor A and Competitor B offer full health benefits; it also reveals that Competitor C offers only limited health benefits.

You may include the information about Competitor A and Competitor B's offer of full health benefits in support of your request for full health insurance—and forgo mention of the information about Competitor C's reduced offering. But, know that the hiring manager may throw Competitor C into the conversation; you must be prepared to explain why you believe that A and B are far more relevant to the discussion at hand.

Within reason, you are also not obligated to present the manager with information you have found that is not explicitly on-point and would otherwise muddy the negotiation waters. For example:

You are interviewing for a starting junior investment banker position at the Dallas branch of a large New York–based firm. In your salary research, you discover that WetFeet's Insider Guide to *Careers in Investment Banking* suggests that the average salary for a starting junior-investment banker is $60,000 and the high-end goes to $75,000. However, WetFeet also states that the salary range for junior investment bankers goes as low as $50,000 at smaller firms outside traditional banking centers.

What is permissible here? Well, remember that the employer can go find and read the WetFeet data themselves, but, if questioned about your choice of data, you should be prepared to defend your mention of WetFeet's average salary and maximum salary information to support your salary demand: Dallas isn't Poughkeepsie and the investment firm is huge.

Before we leave this subject here, we must caution you again to behave ethically as you benchmark and then present the resulting data. Research the market, legitimately differentiate the data that supports your position, keep track of the data that does not support your position, and do *not* present falsified data, unsupported comparisons, or fudged conclusions. If you are in doubt, don't use a piece of data; it is terminal to be thought shady or dishonest.

Discuss Your Salary History Intelligently

It's okay to be open about what you've earned in the past. Honestly answering any questions about your salary history is a good approach—it makes you seem open, and employers can often get the information anyway. You should put some distance, though, between what you have earned before and what is appropriate to the current situation—stress the differences between then and now that merit greater compensation in the new position.

Say you're interviewing for a corporate training position that you think should pay $60,000 to $80,000, but your last job as a Berlitz instructor paid only $40,000. Here's how you might handle the discussion:

Employer: Could you tell me what you were earning at Berlitz?

You: Yes. I accepted a position at only $40,000 because I wanted to develop complete fluency in Spanish, and the schedule allowed me to continue with my human resources program at Whittier College. I'm sure my language ability would be valuable here.

Employer: What would you expect to be earning here at Veratron in this position?

You: I'm sure you've considered what the job involves and will offer a fair salary that is competitive with the industry; I'm relying on that. Now, I would love to hear more about the position's responsibilities. . . .

You are now free to work through your value-increasing strategies.

Here are some additional examples of how to deal with salary history questions:

Scenario A

Employer: You just graduated from college and have been making $9/hour as a waiter. I am sure anything we offer here will be a great improvement over that.

Candidate: Absolutely, but given the fact that I graduated from an excellent finance program with a good grade point average and interned last summer at an investment bank, I am excited to join the professional ranks and earn a professional's salary. Can we talk more about the specific position and its responsibilities?

Scenario B

Employer: We are hiring you into a software programmer position. As I understand it, you are making $40,000 in a similar position at your current employer.

Candidate: Actually, my current title is C++ Programmer, but I recently completed the Oracle database engineer certification program—which is why I am such a good fit for working on your sophisticated database-driven software implementations. Can we talk more about your department's deliverables and how I think I can bring my combined skill sets to bear on those challenges?

Don't Be First to Name a Salary

Notice that the candidates in the previous examples never threw out a specific salary they hoped to earn? This is a key part of your negotiation strategy.

Employers want to get a sense of your expectations as early in the interview process as possible. They will often press you to name a specific salary number or salary range. This is to be avoided for several reasons: If you name a figure in response to a question about your salary expectations, it could be well above what the employer had in mind, and your interviewer's thoughts will shift to another candidate. If the figure is too low, you'll be stuck with less than what the employer was planning to pay—and you may even come off as suddenly less qualified to boot. There is no need to fall into such a trap. The employer knows the responsibilities of the job better than you do and so is better qualified to give it a dollar value. Once that happens, you are in an excellent position to discuss why you could bring more to the position than someone else might.

Let's look at some examples of how to avoid naming a salary first—even when explicitly challenged by the employer to do so:

Scenario A

Employer: Don't you have a minimum salary figure in mind?

Candidate: I have several opportunities I'm considering, and each has different characteristics. I have to take all of the circumstances into account. Maybe you could give some idea of the range for this position?

Employer: Well, let's leave that for later, assuming we decide there's a good fit. Okay?

Candidate: Sure, that makes sense. Why don't we take the opportunity to discuss the position's responsibilities and my background more fully?

Now, back to your value-increasing strategies . . .

Scenario B

Employer: The range for this position is $50,000 to $70,000, depending on experience. Does that fit with what you are expecting?

Candidate: Before we hash out final numbers, could we take a few moments to talk about the job more fully so that I can consider your question? I also wanted to get your take on the recent study on salary trends in this industry that I pulled from the leading trade magazine.

Did somebody say "benchmarking"? Music to our ears!

Scenario C

Employer: The range is $50,000 to $70,000, depending on experience. Can you tell me whether you would accept a salary in that range?

Candidate: I am open to any reasonable offer, but I would like to go over the position's title and responsibilities more fully before agreeing to anything definite.

Scenario D

Employer: The range is $50,000 to $70,000, and we have already interviewed several qualified candidates who have expressed willingness to work at the low end of that range. I don't want to waste either of our time: What salary do you expect?

Candidate: That is great that you have your pick of candidates. I don't want to waste your time either, but let me take a moment to make sure that I have given you a full sense of my own background and skill set—and how I see them plugging into a position of this importance.

Do the preceding topic shifts feel stilted to you? Well, they can certainly feel that way—particularly because the hiring manager may know that you are trying to dance away from fixing a salary number. Don't let that fact stop you from using the above approaches to direct the conversation away from naming a salary and back toward your value-increasing strategies and benchmarked data.

Practice and develop your confidence in using these kinds of approaches in your own voice. And remember that, in most cases, a hiring manager isn't going to drop you from consideration just because you dodge the initial salary questions successfully. In fact, you may have a better chance at winning the job in the end because you have made sure that you had the opportunity to go through your value-increasing presentation first; other candidates who name a salary early in the interview process may never get the chance to present themselves fully because the manager may be turned off after hearing their asking price.

Fielding the Salary Question

Good

"My goal is to join a quality company where I can make a contribution and learn, so the starting salary is less important to me than the opportunity. Can we talk more about what the job would entail?" (You refocus the conversation on the nature of the job.)

"I've looked at salary surveys, and frankly, they're more confusing than helpful because of the differences among the companies in this field—quality, size, location. Perhaps you could tell me how your company values this position." (You paint a picture of yourself as someone who does research and is thoughtful about it, while leading the interviewer to give you information.)

"At this point, I'm most interested in finding a job that lets me use and develop my skills. I'm really excited about your company, and I'm willing to consider any competitive offer." (Also focuses on the job, and confirms your interest in the company without undermining your position.)

"I'm willing to consider reasonable offers." (An obvious brush-off, but the interviewer might let it go.)

Bad

"I haven't really had a chance to give it much thought." (Perhaps you don't give much thought to other important matters, either.)

"As much as you can afford to pay me!" (Okay, this could be funny with the right delivery—if the interviewer has a sense of humor. But even then it's not an effective put-off: The likely response after ha, ha, ha? "Seriously, though . . . ")

"At least $60,000." (The most you'll get is $60,000, even if $65,000 was budgeted. See how naming a figure undercuts your ability to negotiate?)

"I'm expensive, but worth it." (Misguided attempt at humor; sounds clichéd and conceited.)

Note: If the interviewer is so determined to nail you on your salary expectations that you can't proceed with the interview until you name a figure, give a range with a low end that's just above what you think the company's high end will be or better, what the person tells you it is, if you can get that far). That way, the low end of your range and the top end of theirs will be relatively close, you still have some basis for negotiation, and the interview can proceed.

What if it's the HR manager who sends you the offer letter or asks what you would accept? Try the following approach:

You: Thank you for your offer letter. I wanted to let you know that I received it, but I have quite a few meetings scheduled over the next several days, so it's going to be several days before I can give the offer proper attention.

HR manager: Well, can you tell me what your initial reaction is?

He's concerned because of your reference to all those meetings.

You: I still have a few questions about the job's responsibilities and Ron's [the hiring manager's] expectations of me. I'd like to set up another meeting with him to go over those—and also I'd appreciate the opportunity to meet Charlene Osgood [Ron's boss].

You're now positioned to negotiate with Charlene as well, in case she turns out to be an obstacle and the final decision-maker.

HR manager: Fine. I'll ask Ron to get you on his calendar today or tomorrow, if possible. I'll leave it to him to make arrangements with Charlene. When are you available?

Your discussion with the hiring manager should begin with your stated agenda—a review of responsibilities and expectations. This will give you the opportunity to reinforce his sense of your value. Now you can discuss the offer.

As we have seen, there is invariably an advantage to not being the first to name a salary. If you ask for too much, you risk scaring away the employer; if you ask for too little, you shortchange yourself. Of course, many employers will try to pin you down on this near the beginning of the interviewing process to save themselves from considering candidates who are out of range. This seems reasonable enough, until you consider that the employer's view of reasonable compensation for you is subject to change—for the better, once you worked through your strategies to convince the hiring manager that you are the person for the job, increased the perceived value of the job, and, finally, maximized the perceived value of you in the job. You need to buy time to put your strategies into action. Which means you must prepare yourself to resist requests to name your price.

Finally, in the other areas of compensation that are of great importance to you and the employer, you will want to try to practice the same discipline in not naming your specific asking position before you have had a chance to get a sense of the employer's position. Don't waste this technique on terms that don't matter to you or on terms that you suspect don't matter to the employer (i.e., terms aren't at the core of the negotiation anyway).

Continue to Interview Elsewhere

Don't stop developing alternative job offers and identifying hot prospects. You may well find something better, and the process will bolster your confidence and give the impression that you're a person in demand. People wait hours to eat at popular restaurants while less-celebrated spots, perhaps equally good, always have empty tables. The same dynamics apply here. If a competitor thinks well enough of you to make an offer, the company you've set your sights on will probably make an extra effort to snag you.

We know what you're thinking, but inventing alternatives is no substitute for developing real ones. Real alternatives have the ring of truth and allow you to cite specific attractions as bargaining chips. Imaginary alternatives tend to sound phony, and you run the risk that the hiring manager will invite you to take the nonexistent offer. Then you'll have to scramble to find a plausible reason for taking the real job after all, which makes your bargaining position mighty weak.

Knowing that you have real alternatives will also help you ask for what you want with more firmness. You'll be able to walk away from the negotiation without anxiety rather than accept unsatisfactory terms. After all, there's little point in accepting an offer inferior to one you already have—or expect to have—in hand.

What's Negotiable?

- Constraints

- What's on the Table

- Establishing Your Priorities

Constraints

Okay, you have interviewed and you received the offer or are expecting it shortly. It is time to think about what terms are negotiable. . . .

Generally, what's negotiable in a compensation package depends on two key factors. The first is the bargaining power you've built up—by virtue of your successful demonstration of your abilities, the employer's perception of the value of the position and sense of urgency about filling it, and how the negotiations are set up. Most of these factors are somewhat subjective—they depend largely on the hiring manager's mind-set and what you've been able to do to influence it.

The other factor is objective constraints. These are barriers that can't easily be moved no matter what the hiring manager thinks. Such constraints might include

- Union contract terms. If you are signing on as a teacher in a unionized school district, for example, your pay will be predetermined. (But you might be able to negotiate your school assignment, the grade level you teach, and any extra duties.)

- Policies set by the board of directors, such as a formula for determining pay. (But such policies often have loopholes that you can slip through if you have enough bargaining power.)

- Policies set by management, such as not providing allowances. (But you may be able to substitute a different benefit to compensate.)

- Group-hire situations, such as internships, where everyone is paid the same standard salary. (But kickers such as a moving allowance, low-interest loans, tuition reimbursement, time off for pursuing advanced education, and other accommodations may be made for must-have candidates.)

- The pay level of your peers or the person you would report to. This is often a constraint because the manager fears your colleagues will be upset if you get paid more than they do. (But with creative negotiation you can win other forms of compensation and valuable benefits, without setting yourself up for peer-group resentment.)

- The company's financial health or status. An employer that is going through layoffs or bankruptcy may not be able to meet standard market compensation levels. (If you still want to work for the employer, you might demand additional nonfinancial compensation, or a significantly discounted ownership interest in the company, should it turn around.)

As you can see, even with objective constraints, there's often more room for negotiation than you are initially led to believe—if the employer really wants you. To maximize your chances of overcoming barriers, prepare to suggest a situation that's a winner for the manager, too. Consider the following examples:

- "If I attend night school to learn more about operational simulation, could I be of greater value to you, and maybe justify tuition reimbursement?"

- "I know that the school needs to attract students as well as teachers. Could I do some marketing work in addition to teaching? Would that help you meet my salary needs?"

- "Would it be easier for you to use me on a consulting basis, until you're sure I can handle the vendor relationships, and then we can revisit the salary issue?"

What's on the Table

Responsibilities and Opportunities

The starting place for thinking about negotiations should be job responsibilities and opportunities, not compensation. This is true for several reasons:

- Discussion of responsibilities and opportunities is what gives you access to the hiring decision-maker, rather than an intermediary.
- There's a good chance you and the employer will discover that you can make a greater contribution than originally supposed, which may mean better compensation.

Your responsibilities and opportunities will be the most important factor in your job satisfaction—much more than your compensation, if you're paid at all fairly. By clarifying these responsibilities, you'll be able to make a better assessment of whether the position is right for you and to suggest modifications that might make it more appealing.

Here's a sample discussion of responsibilities:

Candidate: Thanks for taking the time to meet with me again. As I said, I'd like to review the responsibilities of the project coordinator.

Employer: Well, I'd want you to keep tabs on the various elements of the project, identifying any roadblocks and bringing them to my attention and tracking project expenses.

Candidate: I can certainly do that. And I assume you'd like me to use project-planning and spreadsheet software and to make appropriate slides for management presentations?

Accepts the job requirements, then makes suggestions for how to increase the value of the work.

Employer: Yes, that would be very helpful. I wasn't sure how comfortable you were with those programs; they are a lot of help in managing a project.

Candidate: Yes, they are. And I hope I can help the staff find ways to overcome roadblocks or delays, so you don't need be involved in issues that can be resolved at a lower level. How does that sound?

Shows understanding of the value of the manager's time and indicates confidence and initiative.

Employer: Great. Just give me a weekly write-up, and come see me if you need my input.

Candidate: Well, I'll certainly do my best to get the project back on track. I know how important it is to the company. Can we review my performance and compensation in the next quarter? I like to know that I'm delivering what's expected.

Shows commitment and accountability—and sets the candidate up for a raise in 3 months.

Employer: I suppose we could arrange for that; I hope to be able to justify an increase at that time, if you do as well as you have asserted is possible.

Candidate: Thanks. One other thing: I may need to work late some evenings to make calls to Asia and start early to reach people in Israel. May I have some discretion in working from home occasionally, as long as I give you an accounting?

Makes a reasonable request, positioning it as a benefit to the company rather than as a personal convenience.

Employer: That shouldn't be a problem as long as we're in good communication and the job gets done.

Candidate: It will. Thank you for discussing this with me.

See how starting with a discussion of responsibilities leads nicely into your requests for other types of consideration (in this case, an early performance review and the flexibility to work from home)? Putting these requests in the proper context makes them much more palatable to potential employers.

Title

Having started with a discussion of responsibilities and opportunities is an excellent lead-in to a conversation about the appropriate title for the position. Now comes your chance to make the case that the nature of the responsibilities and the sophisticated qualifications you bring to the table warrant an expanded or elevated title. And, if you can get your title improved, that can put your compensation discussion on a more advantageous footing.

Let's look at a variation on the previous example:

Candidate: I hope I can help the staff find ways to overcome roadblocks or delays, so you don't need be involved in issues that can be resolved at a lower level. How does that sound?

Employer: Great. Just give me a weekly write-up, and come see me if you need my input.

Candidate: You know, I have the skills and background to not only coordinate project work and reporting, but also to develop initial project specifications and flow-charts for future business. Can I offer to help you in these areas as well?

Employer: That would be quite useful, although I would need to work with you the first few times to ensure that you follow our departmental practices closely when interacting with clients.

Candidate: Absolutely; I am excited to show you what I can do on the project development side. In terms of customer-facing work, it is my experience that it is important that clients feel that they are receiving the appropriate level of attention. I believe that "Senior Project Coordinator" is the title that tends to make clients feel comfortable that the company has placed an experienced coordinator on their account.

Positioning the elevated title as a way to increase customer confidence, rather than as just meeting the candidate's personal professional goals, makes it easier for the hiring manager to agree to. This is an important point: When you can convince the employer that such accommodations benefit the company first, you will find them much easier to attain.

Salary

We repeat: Let the employer name a salary, either verbally or in a written offer letter. Then you can negotiate. You are in a much stronger position to discuss salary when you've done some homework. To get internal data on salary ranges, you may need to tap your inside sources, such as people who interviewed you, people who referred you, or current or former employees. If you know the going rate inside and outside the company, you'll have good justification for requesting a higher salary if the offer falls below either level. Consider this sample dialogue:

Manager: We're impressed with what you have to offer, but we're not sure we can afford you. What are your salary expectations?

Candidate: I need to take into account a number of factors, including the job responsibilities, the learning opportunity, and the working environment. So I'm not set on a specific figure. Can you tell me what you think would be fair and reasonable for what I bring to this position?

Manager: The position, as we've defined it, pays in the range of $50,000 to $70,000, depending on experience.

Candidate: Hmm . . . $70,000 is somewhat below what I've found to be typical in the industry for a position of this responsibility. I have also spoken with several of the current staff who mentioned salary rates in this department that were above that range. That said, I'm glad to hear that experience figures into the equation.

Manager: Well, there are limits to what I can do beyond the defined range, but I may be able to come up with a little more if I allow for your graphic-design skills. We may be able to save a little on what we're now spending on contract design work.

Candidate: That sounds good. Thank you for offering to look at possibilities. Perhaps you can put your best offer into writing so I can give it serious thought.

Avoid naming a salary and let benchmarking/research bump the conversation entirely out of the starting range. Of course, this example assumes that you have data that can be spun to back up your position; if you don't have that data, you can be left looking foolish if the manager either pushes you to produce industry data or happens to know that no one in the department is making more than $70,000.

Signing Bonus

Employers often offer a signing bonus when they can't pay a competitive salary right away or when they're luring someone away from another firm. Because they're not part of the regular payroll, these bonuses are hidden from view—which allows a manager to keep to the departmental salary structure. A signing bonus can range from modest—$1,000 or so—to substantial, depending on how much the firm wants you.

Keep in mind that companies often delay payment of signing bonuses to prevent recipients from collecting the money and then taking off to another opportunity. A common payout schedule is half in 6 months and the balance in 12 months. If you're not satisfied with a company's bonus offer, you may be able to increase it by agreeing to lengthen the payout schedule by a year. This lets the employer push some of your payment into the next budget cycle or even the one beyond that. Just remember: You'll lose any unpaid balance if you choose to leave.

Moving Allowance

A moving allowance is an extra enticement, much like a signing bonus, and depending on the circumstances, you may qualify to receive it tax-free.

Some companies will reimburse you for nearly all moving expenses, including hired movers, temporary living quarters, and sometimes even costs associated with real-estate transactions. Others offer a fixed sum, which may or may not cover all your expenses. The allowance you get is often negotiable, because it's a nonrecurring cost for the company.

Of course, this is only an option when you're interviewing out of your current city or town of residence.

Performance-Based Bonuses and Commissions

Most sales people receive a relatively modest salary, but earn a commission on sales or get bonuses for meeting specified goals. (Sometimes both bonuses and commissions apply). A company's commission and bonus structure may be fixed, but more often it's open to negotiation.

Factors you may want to negotiate include the following:

- Sales goals
- Your commission percentage, standards you must meet to earn it, and additional rewards for exceeding goals
- The size and location of your sales territory, degree of exclusivity, and access to specific accounts
- Length of time you'll be able to keep the territory or accounts if you meet your goals
- Requirements for earning a bonus

You don't have to work in sales to qualify for incentive pay. If the company has a commission or bonus program in place, you may be able to identify measurable goals—such as a bonus or commission tied to the success of a sales team you support—that would qualify you to participate. If the company doesn't have an incentive program, you may be able to design one that's specific to your job.

For example:

- A reward for completing a behind-schedule project on time
- A reward for recovering a business relationship that has gone sour
- A bonus based on measurable improvement in customer satisfaction
- A bonus based on money saved through operational streamlining
- A finder's fee for recruiting needed staff members
- A bonus or commission tied to the number of new customers brought in by marketing programs

The possibilities depend largely on your ability to come up with relevant measures of performance and to demonstrate the value to the business if you reach your goals. This is an area where creative thinking pays off.

Review Date

In most organizations, employees receive annual performance and salary reviews. Even if you haven't been promoted or assigned new responsibilities, you can expect a raise of some amount if your performance is up to standard and the organization is doing even modestly well. An exceptional year may mean bigger raises or one-time bonuses.

Once you've negotiated your salary, you may want to request an earlier-than-usual performance review. If you think you'll be able to demonstrate that you're contributing well beyond your job description, or better yet, to reach agreed-on goals, you may want to request a review after 6 months—or even after 3 months, if you can make a substantial impact that soon.

The value to you can be considerable. Let's say 5 percent annual raises are the norm. A 6-month review that nets you 5 percent puts you in line for a full-year review that will likely result in an additional 2 to 5 percent. This can boost your paycheck thousands of dollars over what you would have received without the early review, and yet, an early review is fairly easy for most managers to grant. After all, good managers prefer early productivity and accountability, especially with new hires.

And, requesting a performance-based bonus demonstrates your confidence in your own work. You're not asking for something for nothing, after all. You're willing to make your bonus contingent on your own performance.

Stock Options

Several years ago, when initial public offerings by companies like Yahoo, Netscape, and Amazon were turning twenty- and thirty-something employees into instant millionaires, everyone wanted stock options. Those go-go dot-com days are over. Still, stock options can sometimes help sweeten the pot. They're most common and potentially lucrative at start-up and early-stage companies. Larger, established companies frequently have option programs; these tend to be less negotiable, offer relatively few shares, and are sometimes restricted to middle and upper management. Options in such cases will rarely make a major difference in your near-term wealth, though after 10 to 15 years they may amount to a good chunk of money.

The number of options granted is more negotiable at early-stage companies. The key to increasing your allotment is demonstrating that a greater ownership position will be an incentive for you to deliver extraordinary value.

This is where those fifth-grade fraction lessons come in handy. There's only so much pie, and you can't expect to get a quarter of it in a manager's position. More likely, you'll be debating over 1,000 shares equal to 0.2 percent of the company versus 1,500 equal to 0.3 percent. Make sure you do the math—10,000 options may sound like a lot, but first you need to know whether the total number of shares is one million or 50 million.

Other considerations: If you're signing on with a start-up, those options will be worth something only if and when the company is sold or goes public. And there's usually a long vesting period before you can exercise your options. So if you're planning on a short stay (or the company decides that's what you'll have), options will be just worthless paper. And, of course, do keep in mind that the vast majority of start-ups never take off.

Tuition Reimbursement and Educational Opportunities

Wouldn't it be great if you could learn a career-advancing new skill or earn an advanced degree on your employer's dime—and even your employer's time? Well, you can.

Tuition reimbursement is a standard benefit that could be worth thousands of dollars. But don't get carried away with fantasies about afternoon art classes—you'll probably have to attend school at night, and you'll need to be learning something the employer believes will help you in your job and thus benefit the company. Be prepared to demonstrate how the courses you plan to take will increase your efficiency, generate ideas, or otherwise make you a more valuable employee. Some employers make loans rather than tuition grants and then forgive part of the loan for each year you remain an employee after concluding the education. Try to arrange for the balance of any loan to be forgiven if you are laid off.

Your employer may also sponsor educational opportunities ranging from informal, on-the-job learning and mentoring to formal programs involving regular courses and seminars. Eligibility for company-sponsored training can be a great perk, especially early in your career.

Recruiters say prospective hires can score major points by expressing an interest in continuing education—a benefit that may not cost much, but that is good for both the company and the employee.

Profit-Sharing and 401(k) Programs

There are two forms of profit sharing. One is a form of incentive pay based on the company's performance. You and the company agree that a percentage of your compensation will be based on the firm's overall profits or profits from certain deals. The other is pension profit sharing, in which the employer contributes a certain amount to your pension plan each year—usually figured as a percentage of your salary—based on the company's profitability.

A 401(k) plan lets you have the company set aside a portion of your pretax income (up to a legal limit) in a tax-deferred investment account. Many employers will also kick in full or partial matching contributions. In principle, the money is supposed to remain in the account until you retire, but certain plans let you borrow against it or make early withdrawals to cover expenses defined as critical, such as buying a home, paying your kids' college tuition, or medical care. Pension profit-sharing and 401(k) plans must conform to government regulations, so their terms are not negotiable. They are worth considering, though, when evaluating job alternatives.

Health Insurance

Company-sponsored health plans vary widely, and many smaller firms don't offer any form of medical insurance. The provisions of the plans won't be negotiable. Expect to pay at least part of the premium yourself (the days of free-ride insurance are over), and look for your employer to offer at least two options—a managed-care plan or HMO and a more traditional fee-for-service plan with a higher copayment.

While you can dip into your after-tax income to buy health insurance or join an HMO, it's obviously better to have your employer pay part of the premium and take your contribution from your pretax earnings. Before you decide to accept a job offer without health coverage, you should factor in the cost of purchasing insurance, unless you enroll in your spouse's company plan. You may be able to persuade the employer to reimburse you for the cost or pay you a higher salary to compensate for the lack of health coverage.

Work Schedule

Your work schedule is usually decreed by the corporate norm, and you'll want to know what it is before you sign on. Although 9-to-5 jobs still exist, 8-to-6 jobs are more common. What can you do if the normal schedule doesn't suit you? You may be able to negotiate a flexible schedule or permission to work at home 1 or 2 days a week. Just be aware that, in either case, your colleagues— and your manager—will be on the alert for any signs that you're slacking off, so make sure the work gets done. You may be better off proving yourself first and then negotiating a special schedule. If you find yourself working long hours that go beyond the corporate norm, you may be able to negotiate comp time— generally, an hour of time off for each hour of overtime. Many companies will even let you cash in unused comp time at the end of the year. Just make sure you have good documentation.

Vacation Time

Most U.S. companies determine paid vacation time by a formula based on how long you've been with the company—say, 2 weeks for the first 3 years, with an additional week tacked on at 4 years and another at 10. This may be negotiable, however, especially if most of the people in your department or at your level are eligible for more than the minimum vacation or if you agree to take your time off at 15- to 20-week intervals, so your excess allotment isn't apparent. You may also be able to negotiate additional time off if you're willing to take it without pay.

Be cautious in this area, though: If you make vacation time the first item on your negotiating agenda, the employer might start to wonder about your enthusiasm for the job. It's best to address time off as more of an afterthought.

Severance Pay

Mergers, acquisitions, disappointing sales, natural disasters—all can lead to layoffs, and even stellar performers can find themselves ushered out the door. Newcomers usually get meager severance pay, so you may want to negotiate a commitment for a better send-off—say, 3 months' pay—if your employment is terminated through no fault of your own.

This should be the last thing you discuss in your negotiations. Termination is regarded in many circles as corporate death, and it's a subject many people would like to avoid. When you do bring it up, treat it as a conjecture: "What if the company were bought, and the new owner decided my job would be perfect for his unemployed nephew? What would I get in the way of severance pay?" Severance pay tends to be a more acceptable subject at companies where a merger or acquisition is rumored to be on the horizon or where the company has been through a major reorganization or bankruptcy recently.

Finally, get the deal in writing—your manager may be laid off too!

Establishing Your Priorities

Your first thought after considering all these options may be "I want it all!" Ask for everything, though, and you may end up getting nothing. A long list of requests and demands—flextime, comp time, special bonuses, extra stock options, a higher-than-usual salary—looks like the sign of a high-maintenance employee, which could give the hiring manager cold feet.

Sit down and really think about what matters to you. Is it salary? Title? Vacation time? Travel? You're better off concentrating on the two or three things that matter the most to you and considering other options only as part of your decision matrix for evaluating offers.

Develop a Negotiation Range for Each Priority

Once you have a sense of all that is available to you from the employer, benchmarked the important details, and established your priorities, it can be quite helpful to create a negotiation range for each of your priorities. Start by identifying the following for each negotiation issue: (1) asking point, (2) walk-away point, (3) relevant data points.

Asking Point

An asking point is the realistic starting demand you will make on a negotiation issue (e.g., salary, benefits, title). Think of your asking point as the best possible outcome for that salary/benefit item that you could hope for in a reasonable world.

For example: You know that the maximum industry salary paid for your skill set and the position you are interviewing for is $60,000 and that is paid by the top companies, who are located in New York City. You are interviewing with a midsized company, located in Charleston, South Carolina. Now, you can guess that such a company, located in an area with a low cost of living, is going to pay at least $10,000 less than big New York employers. Even so, it might not be unreasonable for you to set your salary asking point at $75,000 because it is not completely unreasonable and can be nominally defended with benchmarked market data.

Remember that asking for more than you expect to get creates room for negotiation. Yes, occasionally you will discover that an employer wants you so badly that it will meet your initial demands. More commonly, however, you will find yourself trading down from your initial asking terms while the employer trades up from its starting position. This is normal and even to be encouraged: Trading consideration lets each party feel that it has won concessions from the other side—do not underestimate the value of providing face-saving trades to the other side.

To ensure that you prepare a fully fleshed-out set of asking terms, set aside some time to think about all of the areas of compensation, title, and responsibilities at the new job and develop an asking point for each of your priorities.

Walk-Away Point

Just as you should identify your asking point for each significant negotiation priority, you should take the time to consider the lowest salary, title, responsibilities, and perks that you would accept to do *this* job; these will become your "walk-away" points. This is not a list of your wants, it is a realistic list of your fundamental needs—if you don't achieve that minimum amount/level on each issue, you will walk away from the employer and look for a position elsewhere.

Everyone's walk-away list is different: An established businessperson in the middle of his or her career, with a family and mortgage, is going to have a much more sophisticated set of walk-away terms than a first-time job-seeker entering the workplace. The point here is to set a few important stakes in the ground, beyond which you are not going to let yourself be pushed, period.

The list of walk-away terms you establish will serve as the floor for your negotiation with the employer: Under no circumstances will you accept a final offer that does not substantively meet your walk-away requirements. This is not to say that you must have increases in each area over your previous jobs. In fact, it may be that you are switching professions or trying to find employment in a contracting sector or economy; if so, you should be aware of the impact of those limiting factors on your salary and benefit expectations and on your walk-away terms.

To ensure that you have the most realistic and helpful statement of your walk-away points, ask yourself several questions:

How much do I need to live on? This amount is different for each person, but you may use your monthly spending over the previous 12 months to establish the spending level to which you are currently accustomed. This is not to say that you might not be able to live on less (or more), but you should use the trailing year's numbers as the baseline against which you add or subtract your actual needs.

Finally, don't forget to add on any costs you will incur as a result of the new job—commuting expenses, wardrobe expenses, and so on. Your pay should cover those as well.

How much do I need to do this job? It is important to feel that you are adequately compensated for your work. Think about the relationship between the responsibilities and challenges of the position and what amount of compensation (financial and nonfinancial) will get you out of bed every day and going to work without dread.

This analysis is particularly important where you bear additional risks in your employment; depending on the job, you may be subject to financial risks (e.g., personal legal liability), physical risks (e.g., injury, illness, accident), and emotional risks (e.g., high levels of stress). Some would argue that all of the preceding risks can be quantified and financially insured. Perhaps, but at a minimum you should feel that the financial and nonfinancial rewards of the job are commensurate with the risks you are asked to take.

Finally, it is reasonable to assume that your sense of the market rate for the position and your skill set will sneak into your analysis of how much you need to do the job. That said, try to be aware of that influence and question yourself honestly about what *your* particular needs are. It may be that you can happily do the job for less money and fewer benefits than the other candidates competing with you for the job; for highly price-sensitive employers, this may be the deciding factor in your being hired over the rest of the field.

What title must I have to keep my career on track? Your personality, ambition, peer level, and the constraints of your profession all come into play here. Think about whether title matters to you and your profession. If it does, ask yourself what possible titles fit into your plans for your career. This doesn't mean that you insist on a title bump with each new employer, but it does mean that you are thinking about which titles would help your career and which would set your career back unnecessarily.

What responsibilities do I need to keep me interested and growing in my career? Boredom can be just as stressful as having too much work. Ask yourself what sort of challenges you will require to keep you happy and contribute to your professional development.

What other things do I have to have to be able to take this job? Are there any requirements that are peculiar to you and your situation? These could be anything from handicapped access to college-loan repayment to country club membership to additional life insurance. Be realistic, but get all of these needs down on paper where you can evaluate them seriously.

Putting the Points Together

Now that you have an asking point and a walk-away point for each of your priorities, let's look at how you can develop a negotiation range for each priority, and then add in your research and benchmarking data points. In the following diagram, a sample negotiation range is created for your salary negotiation. First, your salary asking point, $72,000, and walk-away point, $55,000, are marked on a continuum. Then, any additional relevant data points are noted on the continuum.

In this case, the hiring manager proposed a salary range of $50,000 to $60,000 during the interview process. You also found out from a friend who works at the company that similar employees are currently making $62,000 to $67,000. Finally, you researched the market and benchmarked the standard salary for this position and your background at $60,000 to $70,000.

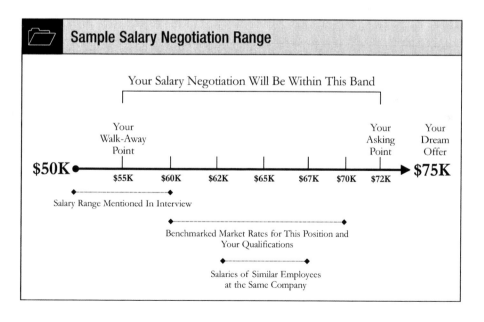

Notice how neatly this continuum frames the coming negotiation? This exercise sharpens the mind like no other—use it to identify

1. Where your asking point seems extreme, weak, or unfounded.

2. Where your asking point seems too low.

3. Where your walk-away point is higher than any data point, meaning you will be making your salary case without any empirical support (not terminal, but typically a much more difficult negotiation).

4. Which data points to use first to support your asking point, and then which data points to use to defend against downward pressure from the employer.

Note: If you find negotiation ranges useful and you are comfortable working with them, you can go one step further and compare your negotiation ranges for different priorities to better identify where, in the negotiation, you might be willing to trade down on one range so that you could move up on another.

Finally, you will often find that your asking point and walk-away point for a negotiation term are exactly the same—meaning there is no room for negotiation on that term. This is not to say that you would not trade other compensation to achieve your fixed goal for this term.

Sweetening the Pot

We have talked primarily about what's negotiable from the employer's side, but you should also consider whether there are any pot-sweeteners that *you* could offer in a pinch. Pot-sweeteners are additional benefits that you could offer the employer that aren't necessarily in the job description. While it is likely that you will use most of these to secure the job offer in the first place, there may be some things you would be willing to throw into the negotiation to secure more compensation and benefits.

Some examples:

- Extra hours
- Additional responsibilities.
- Seeking extra education/certification on your own time
- Investing your own money in the company (typically relevant only to start-ups)

Obtaining the Offer

- Discourage Premature Offers

- Proper Offer Forms

- Benchmark the Offer

- Taking Stock: Create a Decision Matrix

- Assess Your Bargaining Power

Discourage Premature Offers

You've built up your bargaining power, assured that the employer's initial offer will come in on the high end, and determined your negotiating priorities. Now it's time to talk money—and maybe a few perks. Ideally, the offer will come at just the right time—after you've had enough discussion for the employer to get to know and respect you and for you to get a good reading on the job, the company, your manager, and your colleagues. If you're in the enviable position of Most-Wanted Candidate, though, the offer may come too soon, before you're certain the job suits you and before the employer recognizes the position's full value. In this case, you can discourage a premature offer with a conversation like this:

Manager: I've looked over your resume, and from what you've done, I feel you'd do well in the finance manager job. We can offer you $75,000 a year, with a $5,000 starting bonus. How does that sound?

Candidate: Well, we really haven't talked much about the job and how it relates to the company's success. Could we start there?

Sometimes the opposite happens—discussions seem to go on and on, yet no offer is forthcoming. Maybe there's some nagging concern they have about you, and they're reluctant to address it directly. Maybe they can't agree on the necessary qualifications. Maybe their business has taken a dive, and they won't confess it to an outsider. Maybe they're hoping for a miracle person to walk through the door, and you're the fallback candidate. In this situation, if you really want the job, just go for it:

Manager: Nice to see you again, Ellen. My staff members say they enjoyed meeting you.

Candidate: Thank you—that's good to hear. I hope you won't think I'm being pushy, but I really would like to know if there's a job offer forthcoming. While this job is particularly appealing to me, I do have several other prospects, and I need to know how to allocate my time.

Manager: Oh, yes. We're serious. We just want to be sure everyone has met you and that we feel comfortable that it's a good fit—for your own sake, as well as ours.

Candidate: Can you give me an idea of why you're not sure that I'm the right candidate?

Manager: Well, one or two of my people are worried that you don't have an engineering background and might not relate well to such a technical product.

Candidate: I'm glad you brought that up, because I think I can satisfy their concerns. I worked in an electronics lab part-time during the year I graduated, so engineering thinking comes naturally to me. And although my degree is in oceanography, I studied physics and chemistry as well—I have a general science background. Is that helpful?

Manager: Yes, very much so. I'll make the team aware of that, and if everyone is satisfied, I'll have an offer drawn up.

Proper Offer Forms

You may have already had a discussion of proposed salary and compensation specifics—and even received a verbal offer. You may receive the initial offer verbally or in writing—in many cases a verbal offer is a natural development in the conversation—but you should never negotiate terms seriously before you have a written offer in hand. Verbal agreements are much easier than written ones for an employer to back away from either before or after you've taken the job.

If the employer doesn't volunteer an offer letter, politely ask for the offer in writing, so that you can give it careful consideration before discussing its terms at length. As long as the initial offer is clear on the proposed terms and is sent and signed by the manager, an e-mailed copy should be acceptable.

Finally, get the offer home so that you can read it carefully for both content and clarity—and at your own pace. Note any items missing from the letter that were offered verbally during your interviews. Consider the language used to describe each term: Is the language clear? Could reasonable people differ in their understanding of what is describes? Keep track of missing and unclear items and make sure that you bring them up in your negotiation.

Benchmark the Offer

If the offer contains items that you haven't benchmarked previously, or if it is missing items that you expected to find as a matter of course, now is the time to do the additional research and benchmarking necessary to round out your negotiation preparation.

The nice thing about benchmarking at this stage is that you should know exactly what kinds of data you are looking for. Identify the terms you know you want to push on and then really explore the full range of relevant market data points available for that term. As you benchmark, think about what drives the differences in market valuations for that term and how you can manipulate those drivers to assert or defend your negotiation position. Put simply: Figure out what other companies (or the same company) are offering for similar positions, skill sets, and work histories, and come up with cogent arguments for why your situation is most similar to the highest-earning situations and least similar to the lowest-earning situations.

Taking Stock:
Create a Decision Matrix

Now is the time to assess the offer's terms against the priorities and preferences that will define your happiness in a new job. Based on the additional knowledge you've gathered—interviewing with more firms, finding out more about your top choice—since establishing your priorities (see the first chapter, "Before You Interview"), decide whether you want to change your priorities or introduce new ones. One way to get a clear picture of how a single offer compares with your dream job—or how competing offers compare to one another—is to develop a decision matrix.

To create your own decision matrix, start by rating the relative strength and attractiveness of the offer in each of your priority areas, ranked on a scale of zero to ten. Then, multiply the relative weight for each priority factor by the rating you gave the company's offer on that factor. For example, if you gave salary a relative weight of 25 and rated Company X's salary offer at six, Company X would receive 150 points for salary. Add up the results for each factor, and you'll have a score for the offer out of a possible 1,000 points. Generally speaking, you should not have to settle for an offer that scores less than 700 points. This exercise will help you to stay focused on the factors that are most important to you, identify your main negotiating points, and recognize when you should probably look elsewhere.

The sample decision matrix on the next page shows how one job seeker weighted her own preferences, giving each a percentage—and recognizing that some preferences are essential priorities and others are just nice-to-haves. She looked at three job offers and ranked each area of preference for each job on a zero-to-ten scale. Job C had the highest overall score, but Job B was a close second. In fact, Job B might be the better choice because it scored higher in the "Essential" category.

Sample Decision Matrix				
Factor	**Weight (Relative to 100%)**	**Offer's Rating (on a 0–10 scale)**		
		Job A	**Job B**	**Job C**
Essential	**(75%)**			
Growth Opportunities	25	6 (=150)	9 (=225)	8 (=200)
Great Colleagues	15	7 (=105)	8 (=120)	6 (=90)
Challenging Work	15	5 (=75)	10 (=150)	8 (=120)
Travel Opportunities	10	3 (=30)	7 (=70)	9 (=90)
Compensation	10	9 (=90)	5 (=50)	7 (=70)
Nice to Have	**(25%)**			
Reasonable Hours	9	7 (=63)	3 (=27)	4 (=36)
Rapport with Supervisor	9	9 (=81)	5 (=45)	8 (=72)
Recognition	5	8 (=40)	4 (=20)	6 (=30)
Medical Benefits	2	2 (=4)	0 (=0)	2 (=4)
Total	**100%**	**638**	**707**	**712**

The decision factors you settle on should dictate your negotiating priorities. There's no sense in negotiating for something that's of little value to you. If you're a workaholic, why ask for more vacation time? Maybe child-care assistance or overtime pay would be more useful to you.

Next, take stock of where you stand with all your prospects. Is the job you're now negotiating your top choice, or is there another opportunity you'd prefer? Is this your only job offer so far? Are there others in sight, or have all your other prospects fizzled?

If you're blessed with lots of prospects or have just started your job search, you're in a stronger bargaining position, and you may want to go for more money and some nice-to-have factors. If this is your only serious prospect and you've been looking for a while, you might want to proceed with care. Keep in mind, though, that a thorough job campaign may not produce many offers at the outset but tends to yield multiple offers later on, when all the contacts you've made and meetings you've had start to bear fruit.

Assess Your Bargaining Power

If you've done a good job of building your perceived value and uniqueness and have convinced the employer of the need to hire you right away, the initial offer may be much better than what the employer—or you—originally had in mind. And you may be able to make the offer even juicier by employing the tactics outlined in the next chapter, "The Negotiation."

But just as you shouldn't underestimate your bargaining power (you don't want to shortchange yourself), it's important not to overestimate it. To overestimate is to court resentment and lead the employer to search for someone less trouble-some. Your tactics throughout the hiring process should reflect, as accurately as you can assess it, your actual bargaining power.

Some situations are inherently strong. Others have built-in weaknesses. Also, your bargaining power may shift during the course of your interactions with the employer. Another good candidate enters the picture; your bargaining power declines. The employer's need to fill the position grows more urgent; your power increases. The company decides it needs someone with more experience than you to jump in at full speed; your power drops again. You perform admirably on a short-term project; your power grows. You flub it—sorry, your power vanishes. When the situation changes, you'll need to adjust your tactics accordingly.

If someone recommended you for the position or there's a recruiter involved, he or she may be able to tell you what's going on. But you need to learn to read the cues. Frequent calls, requests for references, and hopeful inquiries about your interest are all good signs. Phone calls unreturned for days, interviews repeatedly rescheduled, and vague put-offs don't bode well.

To avoid getting to this point, try to resolve any likely reasons for doubt early on. A less-than-glowing reference is better explained before the reference is checked than after. If someone on the hiring team raises an objection (too little employment continuity, the wrong kind of background), it's better to bring it up and discuss it, rather than let it eat away at your bargaining power. Refer to "Spin the Negatives" in the second chapter, "Negotiate the Interview Process," for tools to deal with negatives.

📁 Bargaining Power

Stronger	Weaker
You were strongly recommended.	You came in through a job posting.
You enter the picture when there are few or no other candidates.	You enter the picture when there are many candidates
You have lots of relevant experience and accomplishments.	You have limited relevant experience or accomplishments.
Your discussions focus on the job.	Your discussions focus primarily on your qualifications.
You've done a good job of building your perceived value.	You've left it to the employer to assess your value.
The employer is concerned about your taking a job elsewhere.	The employer is unconcerned about your going elsewhere.
The hiring manager checks in with you frequently and answers your calls quickly.	Your phone never rings, and your calls are taken by an assistant.
They call to make sure you received the offer letter—and that you like it.	There's little or no follow-up on the offer letter.
They are courting you and give special attention to your feelings about the company.	There's no courting or concern for your feelings about the company.
They mention attractive extras such as a good signing bonus, stock options, and a generous moving allowance.	They seem to have a take-it-or-leave-it attitude.
You have attractive alternatives and are not worried about your prospects.	You're feeling desperate and afraid of losing this opportunity.

Note: You should make some allowances if the hiring manager appears to be dealing with urgent business or is just disorganized and inefficient. Don't give up too easily! Constructive persistence—not nagging—can pay off.

The Negotiation

- The Fundamentals

- Potential Approaches

- The Employer's Bag of Tricks

- Advanced Negotiation Techniques

The Fundamentals

Always Negotiate with the Decision-Maker

You've just negotiated an excellent price on a new car and are ready to sign on the dotted line. Then the salesman tells you he has to clear everything with the boss and disappears into a back office. The boss (who remains faceless) sends word that he can't possibly go that low—his invoice price is just $100 less, not counting transportation charges. The salesman made a mistake. But he could do the deal for another $450, just to cover the transportation cost. He'll pay for your first oil change. What can you do? You've burned through most of your Sunday already, and you want to drive home in that sports car!

A repeated word to the wise: Don't deal with intermediaries in your job negotiations, lest you end up in a similar situation. Intermediaries—human resources representatives, staffing specialists, recruiters, or occasionally someone designated by the hiring manager—usually don't know as much about the job as the person you'll actually be working for, nor do they have the same concern about losing you if the negotiations go astray. They have a lot less latitude to take special circumstances into account. And they're often unaware of what can be done creatively—flexible working hours, extra vacation days, a signing bonus, or company-furnished laptop—to sweeten the pot.

Ask Probing Questions

Probing questions can be lifesavers. You can use them to set a trap for the hiring manager. You can use them to disarm the other side when they are presenting a position that isn't supported by your benchmarking data or information from other interviews. You can use them to buy yourself time to think. You can use them to get the hiring manager talking about a subject she is very comfortable with—or about a subject she isn't very uncomfortable with.

Here are some examples of each approach:

Candidate: Could you walk me through how you arrived at the 8 percent sales commission you are offering me?

Meanwhile, you know from the other employees you interviewed with that everyone in the sales department receives 10 percent.

Candidate: Your job posting was emphatic about salary levels being industry-competitive. Could you take a look at this industry salary data I downloaded from Monster and help me understand how your offer slots into the industry figures?

Your new best friend, benchmarking.

Candidate: Before we talk about the 2 weeks vacation you offered, could you tell me a bit about how vacation time is authorized and accounted for at this company?

Buying time to think . . .

Candidate: I noticed that your department led the development of SQL database-friendly e-mail software. What was involved in that project?

You know from interviewing that the subject is the hiring manager's proudest achievement; your question lets him show off his knowledge and gets him comfortable with you.

Candidate: I met with the CTO yesterday. She mentioned your department is working on developing bulk-mailing software that will work with the sales department's SQL sales target database. What is involved with that project and how is it going?

You know from the CTO that the project is long overdue and the company is losing large numbers of sales to its SQL-integrated competitors; your question knocks the hiring manager out of his comfort zone. This can be useful where the hiring manager is bullying you through the negotiation process.

Get Comfortable and Keep It Simple

Focus on seeming at ease and professional. To ensure you are comfortable when negotiating in person, it is generally best to sit across the table or angled across two contiguous sides of the table; try to avoid sitting on the same side of the table. Do not try to employ negotiation tricks that involve seat height, changing of location, the upper hand in handshakes, or other attempts at nonverbal physical intimidation. These are not usually effective and can turn off a hiring manager quickly. Work on maintaining eye contact and smiling easily during interviews and negotiations. Those two skills will get you far further than gimmickry.

If you do feel that you are often overpowered in negotiations, sit down ahead of time and develop a script for each of your points and include possible hiring manager responses—followed by your replies to those responses. Treat each area separately and practice working through each of your points and replies aloud. Practicing each negotiation point independently will better prepare you for switching topics and arguments naturally as the negotiation proceeds.

While not a trick per se, watching the other side carefully for contradictory facial expressions and vocal tones during a negotiation can be valuable if you are skilled at noting and interpreting that information to your advantage. A sophisticated reference on how to identify nonverbal cues is *Telling Lies: Clues to Deceit in the Marketplace, Politics, and Marriage*, by Paul Ekman.

Creating Win-Win Situations

A job negotiation should generally involve give-and-take—no one likes to be beaten back completely. And, where possible, a win-win negotiation style should be employed in job negotiations: Suggest solutions that are mutually beneficial, that are less costly for the firm, or that let you meet each other halfway. Find trades and develop arguments that let the hiring manager feel good about the final outcome—namely, that the employer is getting more than the employer gave away. The best negotiator positions his arguments so that the other side always feels that meeting the negotiator's demands will be well worth the trade.

The only time that this may not hold true is where the hirer has unreasonable expectations driven by either faulty information about the market value for the position or another qualified candidate exists who is pricing themselves below your walk-away requirements. In the former situation, you must reset the employer's expectations by demonstrating the correct market valuation for the position (via benchmarking!). In the latter case, you will need to stress the added value that you will bring to the position—by reinforcing the value-increasing arguments you made earlier about the value of you in the job.

Pick Your Battles to Win the War

Explicitly and implicitly in any job offer, there will be terms that matter greatly to you (i.e., your priorities) and terms that are not quite so integral to your future happiness in the position. Sit down and divide the parts of the offered package into these two groups. Where possible, you will want to structure your negotiation points so that you trade your concessions on less important items for the employer's concessions on the terms that are more important to you.

Best of all worlds is the situation where the forms of compensation that matter most to you are those that matter least to your prospective employer. In such a case, you can trade compensation terms that don't have much value to you, but that the employer values highly, for compensation terms that the employer values lightly, but that you value greatly. For example:

> You are a procurement specialist and interviewing for a new job . . .

> You have two young children and your spouse works full-time during the week. You are currently spending $300 per child per month on childcare and never see your children during the day.

> Your prospective employer has an on-site childcare facility that charges employees only $100 per child, but has a 12-month waiting list.

> The prospective employer's peculiar inventory system must be audited every Saturday morning. The employer is currently paying a consultant to come in just on Saturday mornings to handle the audit process.

In this example, the hiring manager might happily use some of her political pull at the company to move your children up on the waiting list if it meant that she could drop a high-cost consultant from her department's expense line. And you would happily give up a Saturday morning to decrease your childcare costs dramatically and be able to see your kids everyday during breaks at work.

As you are interviewing and formulating your asking terms, you should be on the lookout for these types of mutually beneficial trades. They are not always readily apparent at first and may need to be teased out with smart, probing questions and follow-up.

Of course, would that every negotiation consisted of win-win exchanges! Unfortunately, the chances are that you will have asking terms that just can't be met by trading away your low-value items for the employer's high-value items. This is where the real friction of negotiation occurs and where you must choose your battles carefully. Stick to negotiating your top priorities first and hardest. Don't get distracted by protracted discussions of nonessential negotiation points; the hiring manager has limited attention span and patience. Eyes on the prize!

Once you have identified your top priorities for negotiation, select the appropriate response(s) to drive the bargain. Let's now look at possible response approaches and their best application . . .

Potential Approaches

You've received an initial offer. Maybe it's everything you want—even beyond your expectations. You'd be happy to accept it as is, right now. Our recommendation: Resist the temptation. You don't want them to think they were too generous. You might indicate that you're generally pleased with the offer, but would appreciate an early performance review, tuition reimbursement, or some other extra that won't be a deal breaker. This will leave your manager thinking he offered you just enough, but not too much. Once your final request is settled, you sign and prepare to start working.

But even if you've made all the moves designed to produce a superior initial offer, chances are there will be some gap between what you're offered and your asking terms. (All that effort at impressing your future employer also boosted your own estimation of your worth!) Or, perhaps, the offer comes in below one or more of your walk-away terms. In either case, here's where the serious negotiation begins.

Let's start by considering the effectiveness and appropriateness of various potential responses to the offer's suggested terms; note that all of the responses in this section may be softened successfully with an introduction such as

- "I appreciate your thinking here . . ."
- "Thank you for taking the time to walk through this with me . . ."
- "I can understand how important this is to the company . . ."
- "I am excited to chat about this with you . . ."

You might use any, and even all, of the following responses in a single offer negotiation. And as you consider the appropriate response for negotiating a particular term—or the appropriate response to counter a hiring manager's response—remember your priorities and be sensitive to the temperature of the room. Don't wear out the hiring manager's patience by presenting complex arguments for your lesser priorities at the beginning of the negotiation.

Avoid the Counterproposal Gamble

Starting your compensation negotiation by countering the employer's offer with an explicit salary proposal is a high-stress opening gambit. It puts you right into the position of haggling and deprives you of the opportunity to "coach" the company to an even higher number. Let's look at an example of the high-risk direct counterproposal:

Employer: Well, you have had time to consider the offer. We feel strongly that an annual salary of $60,000 more than meets industry standards for this position, and fits very well into the generous benefits package we have tendered. We hope that you are excited about the opportunity and ready to come on board!

Candidate: Hmm . . . The number I was actually looking to see here was $72,000. Can you come up to that level?

Employer: I would need to think about that. The maximum we have budgeted for the position is $62,000—and I would have to get the CFO to sign off on that increase and move departmental funds around. If I go through that hassle, will I be certain that we have a deal?

Guess what? You are now stuck in protracted back-and-forth haggling. Naming a counter-salary number out of the gate is just too limiting and even confrontational. And you will find it highly stressful because you will be forced to generate supporting argument after argument to claw your way up from the starting point—which also tends to try the hiring manager's patience and thus close off the number of total issues you can raise in the entire negotiation. For these reasons, we strongly suggest that you avoid making an immediate counterproposal.

The following responses are better bets to get you an automatic improvement on the initial offer—letting you *then* make a counterproposal.

Responses Based on Benchmarking and Research

Here is where the effort you expended on benchmarking, research, and preparation really pays off. A cogent presentation of highly relevant data or information that clearly supports your position, or modifies the hiring manager's assumptions, is the single most effective tool you can bring to a negotiation.

Let's look at some examples of how to use such information to support your contention that you deserve more, often resulting in the hiring manager increasing the offer without first receiving a specific counterproposal from you:

> "I realize that every company is different, but my review of data on compensation for IT systems analysts at local companies employing more than 500 people suggests that average compensation is about 10 percent higher than what you've offered and an upper end about 20 percent higher. I know you want to get the best talent. . . ."

> "From what you've told me, the financial analyst job is really a consulting position, not just an accounting position. A good financial analyst, which I think I am, can save the company hundreds of thousands of dollars a year. I hope you can manage a salary for me that's more in line with consulting—and which I believe would be a fair amount higher than what you've offered. Here are the salary numbers that I pulled from the market . . ."

> "I believe the salary you've suggested would place me at the most junior level in the department. I realize that you're not yet directly familiar with

my work, but you apparently spoke with my references, and I'm sure you found out that I learn quickly and do high-caliber work. Taking these factors into account, I think it makes sense to align me with your midlevel employees."

"As you know, I have a graduate degree in business. I noticed in your other online job postings that candidates with advanced degrees can expect to start at a higher base when working in marketing positions. Given my education and the fact that I will be working cross-functionally with the marketing department, let's talk about a base that reflects that fact. . . ."

Notice how the preceding approaches are more likely to elicit an improvement on the initial compensation offer, to which you can then make a numerical counterproposal? Let's revisit the example from the previous section, but this time after the employer has volunteered an increase in reaction to your data-supported initial response:

Employer (improving on a first offer of $60,000): Well, I guess that given your qualifications and excellent recommendations, we could stretch and go to $66,000.

Candidate (coaching): Thank you for making allowance for my background and experience. And your new offer does bring us closer to what I think I have demonstrated would be fair and acceptable—$72,000 . . .

Candidate (pausing for a few seconds, during which the manager does not seem to have a heart attack at the suggested bump to $72,000): . . . provided we can review my performance in a few months and make an adjustment based on your knowledge of what I can produce.

A request for an early review is one you might plan to make if the negotiation seems to be going your way. If you are having difficulty getting an increase in the base salary, this extra request would be pushing it.

Employer: Well, we only budgeted $62,000 originally, and I have already pushed the CFO hard to agree to the increase to $66,000. That said, I think I would be willing to agree to an early review and a signing bonus of $2,000. If I secure those items, are you ready to agree to a final offer?

Now that we have seen how data-supported responses work for salary issues, let's look at how they can work for other points of negotiation:

Benefits

"Have you had a chance to read the recent *Business Week* article on health insurance benefits at Fortune 500 companies? The article mentions that your COO participated in a panel on the importance of full-time American workers receiving health insurance to guarantee productivity and continuity. . . ."

"My understanding from the consulting reports I have read recently is that the leaders in your industry have recognized that employees working overseas should be provided with additional life insurance. I am excited to work in your Madrid office, but let's discuss bringing my insurance plan into line with that enjoyed by other overseas workers in this industry. . . ."

"According to this Harvard Business School study, administrative personnel who have been exposed to financial accounting concepts tend to be better stewards of company resources. The local community college offers a Friday afternoon accounting class that could help me grow in this position."

Perks

"I can understand why you would not want to blithely authorize trips to annual professional conferences in Aspen. However, let me show you an estimate of the sales numbers that I put up at my last job in the 30 days following each professional conference I attended. . . ."

"Sure, paying a club membership fee may be something the company hasn't ever done before, but did you know that the purchasing manager and CFO at Company X are members of Fair Oaks Country Club?"

Title

"I realize it may not be traditional to hire in a junior business development employee at the title of Manager, but I learned from my interviews with your other staff that they have found that a new deal tends to get on track faster when the prospective partner knows that they are dealing with a manager here."

"This is a new position in a newly formed department and, as such, doesn't have a history here that would firmly dictate a specific title. I took the opportunity to research the title level that typically adheres to customer service managers who are responsible for rolling out phone support for a new software product at similar companies and can demonstrate that Director is the appropriate title for this responsibility."

Responses Based on Your Own Needs

The following are examples of responses you could offer that would be based purely on your own needs:

- "I really need to start several hundred dollars a month higher to be able to make my rent payments."

- "Child care is expensive, as you know. Could you include an allowance for that?"

- "I plan to go to night school in the fall, so I'll have to drop my part-time job. I'm afraid what you've offered won't make up the difference."

- "I have an hour-and-a-half commute, so my transportation costs will be substantial. I had hoped you would be able to pay somewhat more than what I've already been offered by a company near where I live."

Do these pleas make you want to reach for your wallet? Probably not. The hiring manager is also unlikely to be moved and will probably say something along the lines of, "Well, maybe you'd better look for a job that pays better," or "Sounds like you'd better take that other job."

Even if you're in a strong bargaining position and the employer doesn't want to lose you, you've probably shortchanged yourself by requesting coverage of a specific, relatively small item, rather than asking for more based on your perceived worth.

Note, however, that this kind of approach can be useful, near the end of your negotiation, in winning a specific lower-priority item after you've used more fruitful approaches to achieve your main compensation objectives. To make a concession to your needs easier for the manager to swallow, try wrapping it in win-win language:

- "Now that we're in agreement on salary and bonuses, I'd like to bring up one other matter. I have a fairly lengthy commute every day, and want to be able to put in the hours here that the job requires. This will mean some child-care expense that I wouldn't have with a job closer to home. Can you include an amount to cover these costs?"

- "I have only a few units left toward completing my master's degree, but I'll need some daylight hours to do it. Could I compensate for being away at class one morning a week with some evening work, and would you be willing to provide tuition reimbursement?"

You should have also noticed that, while each response is driven solely by your needs, in each of these examples there is an implicit advantage to the company in granting your request: your ability to put in long hours, your ability to apply knowledge obtained in completing a master's degree.

Responses Based on the Employer's Needs

It's usually more effective to define your needs in terms of benefits to the employer. Consider the following examples:

- "It occurs to me that you're hiring me primarily for my skills in running a top-notch kindergarten program. But I know that each additional student means hundreds of dollars a month to the school, and I have ideas for marketing the program to parents of preschoolers and to real-estate professionals. I know I could pursue them without interfering with my kindergarten responsibilities. Why don't we combine the two roles and come up with a great solution for both of us?"

- "My computer graphics and communications skills will certainly help me in my role as a customer service representative. But I believe the procedures manuals could benefit from a simplification. From what I've been hearing, they involve some paths that are no longer relevant and others that are hard to understand. I know you don't have a lot to spend on getting external help on this, but I'm qualified and would be glad to help when time permits. I think this would be of value and justify a higher salary."

- "One way out of this dilemma might be for me to take on operations management of the Opal-lite project as a short-term assignment. Then, when I've had the opportunity to demonstrate that I can get things moving and develop procedures to keep them from getting off track again, we could return to a discussion of the kind of permanent position I could fill here."

This kind of response is particularly effective with entrepreneurial or innovative managers. It suggests a way around a salary impasse, rather than getting into a numbers war. Your effort to understand and satisfy the company's needs enhances your perceived value, thereby opening up the negotiating possibilities considerably.

Responses Based on Finding Creative Alternatives

Often a hiring manager really wants to satisfy you, but she may be subject to constraints that are impossible to overcome. For example:

- The maximum salary authorization is set in stone by the hiring manager's supervisor or the CFO.

- The company has never paid a moving allowance, and it isn't about to set a new precedent for doing so now.

- Your request for flextime will open up a can of worms within the department—half the current staff members have asked for it and been turned down.

In situations like these the manager will probably tip you off with language such as, "Look, I'd really like to be able to give you what you ask, but my hands are tied," or "That's really all I can do. I just can't go any further. I hope you decide to accept." Then it's up to you to accept, decline, or get creative. If you believe the manager is telling you the truth about his hands being tied, you might decide to go ahead and accept or decline based on the merits of the offer and the organization.

However, if you suspect that there is a chance that the manager is trying to arbitrarily close off further discussion by claiming external constraints, be polite, but don't let this kind of pat statement go unexplored. Ask polite probing questions to discover the nature and limits of the constraint. It is not uncommon to discover that the assumptions or logic behind a firm constraint are faulty. For example: You are interviewing for a sales position at a small, but growing company and the hiring manager states that the employer offers a very small commission that is negligible compared to the base salary. After further discussion, you learn that the percentage was set by the CEO, who originally handled most sales himself when the business was starting out. In such a case, if you believe in your sales skills and the product you will be selling, you have an opportunity to walk the hiring manager through the motivating advantages of higher commission percentages to the bottom line—and introduce plenty of market research and supporting documentation to make your argument.

In any case, once you have a good sense of the employer's thinking, look for ways to creatively bypass the constraint:

- You asked for a salary higher than the manager could offer, but a performance bonus or an early review with a predetermined raise tied to defined goals might net you close to the same amount.

- You asked for a moving allowance, but you could use a signing bonus to cover those costs.

- You asked for flextime, but maybe you could solve the problem by working at home during specified hours.

The dialogue might go something like this:

Candidate: So $55,000 isn't a target cap; it's set in stone and there's no way you can pay more?

Manager: That's right. So if you won't take less than $60,000, I don't see how we can hire you. We are going to have to stop the discussion here and wish you well in other opportunities.

Candidate: Well, the starting salary isn't as important as the opportunity. Would you be able to revise the salary more easily later if I meet the goals you and I discussed?

Manager: Yes, I could do that.

Candidate: Then maybe we can agree on a 3-month evaluation, and if I hit the targets we set, we can celebrate by giving me a raise.

Manager: Okay. That's a good way to handle it. Are there any other items we need to cover?

Sometimes the manager will resist your suggestion; if so, try extending your time frame:

Manager: I think that's too soon for us to conclude that your work merits a raise; we're hiring you to do good work in the first place.

Candidate: I certainly intend to do good work, but I hope that you could at least feel comfortable evaluating me within 6 months. Would that be acceptable?

Manager: Yes, I could agree to that.

If the manager turns down your request because it's "just not done here," but you have an example to the contrary, try a diplomatic response like this: "Perhaps I was misinformed or don't fully understand the situation, but I was under the impression that other employees have received help with long-distance moves in the past. Maybe we could use a justification similar to that employed in those cases?" This allows the manager to concede that there are special cases— without having to admit to having misrepresented the situation.

Responses Designed to Create Tension

In some cases, you can use simple techniques to make the hiring manager uncomfortable enough to capitulate and give you more than he originally intended. Anxiety can work in your favor, but be careful. The idea is to create tension that can work in your favor without overdoing it. If you carry this tactic too far, it'll backfire. Here are some examples of where this technique worked:

The manager, who you know has invested several months in the hiring process, has finally settled on you and hopes you can begin immediately. She makes an offer of $85,000. You ask for a few days to think it over. She asks if the salary is the issue. You say that it's certainly a factor. She ups the offer to $90,000, provided you give her an answer now and agree to start Monday. (The advisability of further negotiation depends on the strength of your bargaining position. If it's relatively weak, don't push your luck. But if you know it's strong, you could name a slightly higher figure that would settle the salary issue for you and still leave other areas open for negotiation. Or you could agree to the $90,000 and bring up a signing bonus.)

The manager makes an offer of $75,000 plus 5,000 stock options. You say how excited you are about the company and its prospects. You say the offer is appealing, but a little less so financially than one you received just a couple of days ago from another start-up. The manager asks about the gap, and you disclose that the base salaries are close, but the other company is about twice as generous with its options and has similar prospects. The manager asks to compare what the options are really worth and then increases the offer to 8,000 options, plus 2,000 more for each year you stay with the company. (Worth the anxiety you created—unless you fabricated the other offer and the manager invites you to accept the imaginary offer.)

The manager makes an offer of $49,000. You look unhappy and wait 15 seconds without giving any verbal response. Chances are good that the manager will feel anxious and say something like: "I could maybe go a little higher—say, to 51 or 52." (When's the last time you made $3,000 just for shutting up? Sometimes anxiety on the manager's part can work in your favor, but don't overdo it.)

Do not confuse anxiety-producing approaches with hostility. You should be extremely courteous at all times, particularly when you are talking about a competitive offer or delaying. Take this example:

Candidate: Thank you very much for your offer. You've made it really difficult for me. I'm eager to work here, and I've heard only good things about your department. But financially, this just isn't as attractive an offer as I hoped it would be. On Monday I received an offer from another great company that's somewhat higher. I'll have to get back to you on this.

Manager: Tell me more about the other situation. Maybe we can find a way to do a little better. . . .

 ## Silence Is a Golden Opportunity

In almost every business negotiation there are moments that call for the ability to stay silent—even when your normal social instincts are screaming at you to say something. The most important of such moments and the one that you should be on the lookout for in a job offer negotiation is what you can think of as the *question lurking in a statement.* If you can learn to identify these moments and get through them, you will reap the benefits many times over the course of your career—and not just in job negotiations.

Here are some examples of questions lurking in statements:

Employer: So, we think your resume looks good and the team is excited to work with you. Our current thinking is that it might make sense to start you off at an annual salary of $50,000. . . .

Employer: We would really like to be able to meet your salary demand of $60,000, but the CEO has told me that the investors are pressuring him to keep labor costs down. . . .

Employer: As you may know, our company usually hires new employees on a trial basis at an hourly wage. . . .

Silence Is a Golden Opportunity (cont'd)

Each of the preceding examples ends in ellipses to signify that the speakers either trail off or raise the pitch of their voices at the end of the statements (just as they would when asking a question). These speech clues are clear giveaways that the speakers are trying to elicit agreement from you before they continue. In effect, they are trying to get you to agree to their premise so that further negotiation on that term is curtailed. Do not get sucked into responding automatically to these sorts of open statements. If you are uncomfortable being silent while maintaining normal eye contact, try looking at your materials thoughtfully instead. While you are enduring the silence, focus your concentration on how you would deal with the lingering statement if the hiring manager rephrased it as a direct question—because she may very well do so to break the pause.

When you remain silent in these situations, the onus is on the speaker to rephrase the statement as a direct question. Or—even better—the silence may have the same effect on the speaker that it was intended to have on you: It may compel the employer to speak up because he feels the need to fill the conversational space. In those moments, you will occasionally find that the hiring manager will suddenly up the previous offer or sweeten the perks because of her social discomfort.

Even if the speaker is disciplined and either asks what you think about his statement or rephrases the statement as a direct question, you will have now had the benefit of extra time to prepare your response to his attempt to lower your expectations on an important negotiation point. Most importantly, you will have sent a signal to the hiring manager that he cannot assume a dominant role in the negotiation. This kind of perceived parity will serve you well on the negotiation points that follow.

Silence Is a Golden Opportunity (cont'd)

Finally, it's worth noting that your ability to use silence effectively in an offer negotiation is directly related to how positively you came across during the interview period. If you have personally connected with the hiring manager during the interview process, the discomfiting impact of a pregnant pause on that person during the negotiation will be far greater. Most importantly, choose your silent moments wisely: Look for the speech and context clues that signal the hiring manager's lack of confidence or comfort, while controlling your body and eye movements carefully as you wait patiently for the pause to be filled by the other side. Appearing natural and confident, while maintaining normal eye contact, works best. Avoid nervous smiling, scowling, or sudden changes in body position. The point here is to force the hiring manager to address the uncomfortable silence without distraction.

Responses Designed to Reduce Tension

If you feel like the tension is growing out of control and the hiring manager is on the verge of turning hostile, it's time to back off. The following are some examples of responses that are designed to reduce tension:

- "Maybe I'm being a little unrealistic about what you can do. If so, I apologize. I really want to work here, and I'm just hoping to reach an agreement that seems fair to you and takes into account what I bring to the job."

- "I noticed your reaction to what I just proposed. Maybe that's more than you can do, so perhaps you could tell me what is possible."
  (It's better to invite the person to name a number that's more acceptable than to underbid yourself by suggesting a reduced amount and then having to keep backing off. You'll soon look pretty foolish.)

- "I hope I'm not giving you the impression that I'm not committed to the company. The only reason I asked for all 10,000 shares right away is the way this company is exploding. Can't we work it out so that I'm awarded the 10,000 shares now, but only 2,500 vest now, and the rest vest over 3 years?

That way you'll have a completely motivated employee right away, instead of one who hopes the price of shares doesn't go up too much!"
(Note that this proposal locks in the share price at today's value.)

- "You know, I grew up not far from here and have strong ties to this community. It really would be nice to settle down back here. . . ."
(This is a deflation technique that, properly executed and accepted, can get you away from a confrontational topic entirely for a few minutes while you wax poetic about the area.)

Prepare to Change Your Approach

Some negotiations are concluded in a single meeting. Others may stretch out over a few days and involve several players. You're likely to face many twists and turns in the negotiating process, and you should be prepared to change your approach to suit the situation.

Rushing the discussions could force you to agree to less than you might otherwise achieve or prevent you from receiving a competing offer, which would strengthen your bargaining position. Delaying the discussions, on the other hand, leaves an opening for another strong candidate to appear, reducing your bargaining power.

This is why you need to constantly assess your bargaining power. Remember: If you reach for the stars and your ladder is only moon-high, you risk appearing too demanding or too high-maintenance. If you don't reach at all, you're almost certainly passing up money and benefits the employer would have been willing to grant. And if you know you're seen as a must-have, you can be bold—but never be arrogant. Arrogance will only decrease your appeal. Instead, go to extra lengths to express gratitude for the offer, even when saying no to an inadequate proposal, and suggest that you'll think about what might work better.

Finally, avoid pushing things so far that your final deal will be resented. You may become the victim of over-eager scrutiny, be criticized unfairly, or otherwise find yourself made to feel uncomfortable once on the job. You have to live in the climate you create. Which leads us to . . .

Responses to Avoid

Runaway Ego

Candidate: I don't really need this job, so if you don't make it worth my while, I'm not going to take it.

Whoa! This is likely to really push the manager's buttons—the ones that print out the letter revoking the offer. True or not, this statement sounds like a threat. And if you do end up getting the job despite this gaffe, you'll have quite a reputation to live down.

Showing Off

Employer: Knowing that we don't pay at the top of the industry, why do you want to work here?

Candidate: I really don't need the money. I just like the work.

This kind of response may be acceptable if you're sure others in the work group or the manager are similarly motivated; for example, this might be an effective response when interviewing for a position with a nonprofit organization. Otherwise, in a normal business situation, the hiring manager may wonder how to motivate you—or worse, think you are an insufferable braggart.

Patronizing Manner

Employer: Our offer was $30,000; you asked for $50,000. That is a lot of money for a hotel management trainee.

Candidate: Did you read my resume? You should know that I won't be a trainee for more than a month.

Don't confuse arrogance with confidence.

Showing Your Cards

Employer: Would $80,000 be a good starting figure?

Candidate: Wow! That is fantastic. I thought the offer was going to be much lower.

Keep your cool! Your employer probably knows the typical salary range for a position like this and has made a competitive offer. It does you no good to reveal that you haven't done your homework and that the manager could get you for less.

Employer: Would $40,000 be a good starting figure?

Candidate: I couldn't manage on that, unless I sold my car, which I'd hate to do, because I need it to come to work.

Will the manager have to give you a raise or a bonus whenever you need to see the dentist, too?

Late-Breaking Demands

Employer: I guess that about wraps it up. When can you start?

Candidate: I'm planning to take a vacation in August, and then I'll have some personal business in early September. How about September 15?

Why didn't you bring this up earlier? No one likes surprises from new employees.

Culture Clashes

Candidate: Since my child is in school, is it possible to take off school holidays?

This is touchy. Be sensitive to company culture when bringing up family responsibilities. If the manager tells you she hasn't taken a day off in 2 years, you're better off keeping quiet about this and finding a way to make your standard vacation allotment work. But if the salary is low and the company can't pay you more, this may be negotiable.

Poor-Mouthing Doesn't Work

Inexperienced negotiators often make the mistake of believing that the best way to increase the value they are getting from a deal is to start the negotiations by denigrating the value, quality, or both of what the other side has to offer, also called *poor-mouthing.*

Let take a look at how negative observations are best handled. Consider the following example:

Credible, Inc., is a 200-employee operation that had 300 employees at one point, but it lost ground to competitors and was forced to go through lay-offs—from which it has recently stabilized and is now nominally profitable with growing sales.

Abel, a sales account manager, is interviewing with hiring manager, Baker, at Credible, Inc. Baker runs the sales department and knows she needs to hire a talented account manager to support the recent turnaround in sales numbers.

Baker originally posted the position as starting at $50,000 with a 2 percent commission on all retained accounts. After Abel employed his value-increasing strategies during the interview process, Baker offered Abel a $50,000 base salary with a 3 percent commission on retained accounts.

Abel wants a starting salary of $60,000 and a 5 percent commission on all retained accounts.

Scenario 1

Abel starts to negotiate with Baker by mentioning his surprise at the bad executive decisions made by Credible, Inc., during the decline. Abel indicates that he thinks the company's products are still behind those of Credible's competitors and he suspects there is a good chance that Credible, Inc., could backslide into the red at

Poor-Mouthing Doesn't Work (cont'd)

any moment. Abel finishes by saying that he will need to make at least $60,000 and a 5 percent commission to cover his risk in working at a recently unsuccessful company like Credible, Inc.

In this scenario, Abel makes a very common mistake that can sour a deal early on and should be avoided in every negotiation. By poor-mouthing Credible, Inc., and its management right from the start, Abel has eliminated any possibility of goodwill coming into play during the negotiation. All Abel can hope is that Baker has a submissive personality or really needs an account manager—any account manager. This is not to say that these sorts of negotiators don't exist, but they are fairly rare in the normal business world and you would be well served to avoid the gamble of beginning a job negotiation with poor-mouthing. No manager wants to start a negotiation by listening to disparaging comments about his department, the company, its products, or the hiring position from a prospective employee. You will buy yourself a ticket out the door with this mistake.

Scenario 2

Abel starts to negotiate with Baker by thanking her for the offer—and particularly for showing him around and making him feel so welcome. Abel then makes positive comments about the turnaround Credible, Inc., has recently pulled off—and how Baker must be very proud of her team and its performance under duress. Abel mentions how he (or a friend) once worked at a company that did not handle a downturn well and can appreciate the challenges overcome by Credible, Inc.— particularly because Abel (or Abel's friend) saw his own commission income dramatically affected by his employer's continuing product difficulties. *(His point subtly made, Abel then moves on to standard negotiation techniques, like those outlined earlier in this chapter.)*

Poor-Mouthing Doesn't Work (cont'd)

In this scenario, Abel starts by praising Baker and Credible, Inc., which aligns Abel and Baker. To encourage Baker to empathize with his own position, Abel provides some background on his desire to avoid working for a company with a flagging product line. This is not to say that you should invent sympathetic information—and you should absolutely avoid presenting information that makes you look pathetic—but providing a legitimate personal connection to the complexities of the position can sneak your initial reservations about the employer into consideration without raising hackles the way that blunt analysis can. If necessary, later in the negotiation, after working through his less confrontational tactics, Abel can return to Credible's instability and mention it as a reason why another offer or opportunity is looking more attractive. Bringing this issue up once the negotiation has moved further down field is absolutely fair game; don't shrink from pointing out legitimate negative reasons why an offer from one company is not quite as attractive as another. Our point here is that you should avoid starting the discussion with disparaging assessments and when you do have to bring up the company's negatives later on in the negotiation, try to avoid pejorative language.

Mind Your Manners

You may find yourself frustrated by the slowness of the interview and negotiation process, rescheduled meetings, lack of communication, or brusque responses to your queries. These are indicators of the organization's culture, and you may want to take this into account when deciding whether to accept or reject the offer. But there's never a reason for you to abandon good manners. Politeness will earn you favorable reviews; rudeness never will.

It's possible to be polite even when you're saying no or insisting on obtaining a clearer picture of what's happening. For example: "Pardon me, but I'm unable to arrange my schedule without knowing when I might be able to conclude my discussions with Mr. Harper. People are calling, wanting to know when I might be available, but I'd like to give Mr. Harper priority. Could you talk with him, please, and let me know whether Monday or Tuesday would be convenient for our wrap-up discussion on the possibility of my joining his department?"

How Not to Negotiate

Version 1

Manager: So how much were you thinking about as a starting salary?

Candidate: I've just become engaged, so I'll need a bigger apartment. And we're thinking of starting a family after the wedding. So I need $55,000 to begin with, plus a health plan. (Remember, never be the first to name a figure. And, in any case, personal needs aren't good persuaders, especially when they raise concerns about competing interests.)

Manager: We've never paid anything like that to a beginner! I'm afraid we just aren't speaking the same language.

Candidate: Well, maybe when you were young, families could live on a pittance, but that's not the way I plan to start out. So how much do you think you can afford to pay? (Even without the sarcasm, insult, and pomposity, a strident tone like this is likely to anger the hiring manager; at a minimum, it won't lead to a productive discussion of what you can contribute to the company.)

Manager: (Withdrawing from a relationship that already is souring) I'll have to take it up with my HR people. We'll get back to you. (Probably with a rejection letter.)

Candidate: (Realizing he has said something offensive, but still clueless) I hope you can do some persuading with them. I want to be reasonable, and maybe I could take a little less. . . . (Sorry, pal; it's too late now.)

Manager: (Now focused on getting the candidate to leave) I'm afraid I have another meeting to get to now. We'll get back to you (with a rejection).

Version 2

Manager: So what were you thinking about as a starting salary?

Candidate: I don't know. How about maybe $48,000? (Again, it's a mistake to name a figure in response to this question, and when you do say what you want, make sure you sound like you think you deserve it.)

Manager: (Sounding shocked) We can't possibly pay that much to a beginner. The highest I can go is $38,000. (The manager may not really be shocked; you need to probe more to find if this is really a cap.)

Candidate: (Unprepared for this, and not wanting lose the job) Okay. I hope I can start this coming Monday. (This isn't negotiation. It's capitulation!)

Manager: Good. But I need a little time to check references, prepare an offer letter, and discuss this with my boss. He doesn't always automatically approve paying the top rate and may not go for your limited experience, even though I believe you can do the job. (The manager is surprised that the candidate has accepted—he had reserved some extra money for negotiations. Now the manager is worried the candidate seems anxious and may not be a great prospect after all—time to rethink this.)

Candidate: (Sensing the manager's new reluctance) I can be somewhat flexible, but hope it doesn't go too much below $38,000. (It definitely will now.)

Manager: (Doubtfully) I'll see what I can do.

The Employer's Bag of Tricks

The hiring manager probably has some experience in negotiating, and he or she may be adept at tactics designed to get you to accept an offer or conditions that aren't commensurate with what you had in mind. We describe some of the more common tactics here.

Imaginary Competitors

The hiring manager or recruiter may drop hints that your requests are becoming too onerous and that another candidate—or even several—is waiting in the wings.

This may be true, and in that case you should take heed. Or it may just be a ploy to win your quick acceptance. There's no sure way to tell, but you can inquire about the other person's qualifications. If the person is real, you're likely to get a description, which will allow you to make a value comparison. If the person is a phantom, you'll probably get a vague answer. Depending on your reading of your current bargaining power, you can continue negotiating or accept the offer as final and proceed accordingly.

Delays

You may be jubilant over a series of excellent interviews at Company X and the promise of an offer in the mail. The offer is slow in coming, however, and when it arrives, it's less than you expected. You communicate with the person who sent you the offer and request a meeting. The meeting takes a while to arrange, and then it's postponed. You are getting anxious and may be tempted to accept the meager compensation in the offer letter. Delays can occur for a variety of reasons, and it's not always easy to tell what's going on in a particular situation:

- Something may have changed in the organization's business situation, putting a temporary hold on hiring.
- Something may have happened that affects the job itself, changing the requirements and the type of person who could best fulfill them.
- The hiring manager may be on the way out.
- Another candidate may have entered the picture.

Regardless of the reason, the best way to deal with delaying tactics without undermining your position is to get busy on your job campaign again. Call those contacts, set up more meetings, and make sure your name is out there. Pretty soon options that are equal to or better than what Company X has put on the table will pop up. And then you will have bargaining power, as well as two fine offers.

Is this really the way the world works? Yes. Job offers tend to come in clusters, if you've been active in setting up meetings, networking, interviewing, and doing everything else that goes into a campaign.

Rushing Your Decision

A manager may tell you he must fill the job this week—take it or leave it. The aim is twofold: (1) to gain your quick acceptance of terms you might not otherwise agree to, and (2) to prevent you from exploring other options and finding something better. While there may be some urgency, it is more than likely exaggerated. Most managers will wait a reasonable time (say a week) for you to consider and discuss the offer—if they truly want you.

What can you do to slow things down? Simply say that this is a very important decision and you need a few days to give it the consideration it deserves. This may well result in the manager improving the offer to spur you to an early decision. In this situation you need to consult your decision matrix to get a picture of how this offer compares with your other options.

Accept in haste, repent at leisure.

Promises, Promises

Accepting a job is a bit like getting married. During the courtship period, many promises are made. Depending on your partner, they may or may not be kept.

Some managers will deliver on every detail of any commitment they made while recruiting you. Others will make lots of empty promises. What can you do to protect yourself? First, you should ask about the hiring manager's reputation while you are interviewing for the position. You can do this diplomatically by asking neutral questions of the hiring manager's colleagues, such as, "What do you like best about Tom's management style?" and "What, if anything, do you find not to be as helpful in his approach?" These questions are unlikely to ruffle Tom's feathers if he hears about them—unless he's very insecure, dictatorial, or otherwise difficult to deal with, in which case you probably don't want to work for him anyway. And, if you still want to work for him, at least you now know what you're getting into.

Managers who are prone to misrepresenting prospects, impending changes at the company, or other matters can't be trusted on employment commitments. Second, get the important commitments in writing, as part of your final letter offer. After all, even the most trustworthy managers can be reassigned or leave the company, and their verbal commitments won't mean much when they're gone.

Policy

"It can't be done. It's against our policy." This may or may not be true. Very few policies are observed without exception, and your situation could be an exception. Even if it isn't, there are often routes around unmovable policies— you just have to seek them out. See the earlier discussion in this chapter of responses based on creative alternatives.

Financial Duress

It doesn't make a company look attractive as a possible long-term employer, but if you are interviewing with a small business or a start-up, you may encounter a hiring manager who tells you that the company just can't afford to pay a penny more without real damage to the bottom line. Hopefully, by the time you reach this point, you will have done some research on the industry, the company, and the position, and you will know whether to accept this argument at face value or to push on it with confidence.

If you are unsure or feel pressured, don't be afraid to walk the manager back through your value-increasing fundamentals. This can often shake loose a few extra dollars from an employer claiming penury.

Rudeness or Unreasonable Behavior

For better or worse, personalities drive negotiation style. You will occasionally encounter a hiring manager who resorts to being rude, denigrating your resume or skills, or is just plain unreasonable. When you come across one of these folks, you will first have to take a moment to evaluate whether you want the job badly enough to work for someone whose professionalism is so poor at such an early stage of your relationship. (It is our experience that managers who aren't professional in a job negotiation are often the same managers who tend to make your work life unbearable once you have the job.)

That said, if you still want the job, take a deep breath, stay calm, and continue to make your supporting arguments. If possible, take a break (even just a visit to the bathroom can help) to give yourself some distance to assess what is driving the hiring manager's behavior. Ask yourself:

Could anything in my behavior be triggering the manager's reaction? Am I being loud, aggressive, negative, or physically imposing?

Tune down your presence. Lower your voice. Find ways to reconnect on a personal level before continuing to discuss negotiation points.

Could the manager just be tired?

Ask whether you can take a break or adjourn to allow you to consider the options presented so far. If you do adjourn, be sure, at the time, to schedule a date and time at which to resume the negotiation.

Could the manager suspect I am here to replace him?

State how excited you are to work closely with him; reinforce this message whenever possible. Identify specific areas where you will depend on his skills and help to get your job done.

Is the hiring manager personally eccentric or socially stunted?

This is the toughest of all worlds and may very well be an insurmountable problem. However, this type of person often has a hobby, philosophy, or thing about which they are extremely passionate (even more so than the average person would be). Once you get them on this subject, this type can expound for hours and is happy to have an agreeable captive audience.

For example, if you are interviewing with the eccentric owner of a small business, the thing they will be most passionate about will likely be their business.

As you encourage the owner to tell you all about the business, take every opportunity to briefly compliment the company's organization, products, business plan, and marketing. For this sort of person, whose sense of self is so tied up in their business, such compliments are effectively the same as complimenting them personally. Let the speaker toot on his horn for as long as he has air before returning to pressing your negotiation points.

If you can't figure out the person's passion and they don't react to professional stroking, try to introduce a common interest topic that is as inoffensive as possible. Sports, weather, traffic, and children are the safest topics for business situations. Ask very short questions, listen carefully, and use any opportunity to agree with the hiring manager's opinions and compliment his choices. Again, the point here is to get him talking about a safe subject and to help him see you as nonthreatening and agreeable.

As you can imagine, restoring goodwill in a negotiation with an eccentric or unreasonable manager is a delicate dance and often fruitless, but, if you just have to have the job, the above approaches are your best shot to get back to a level playing field as quickly as possible.

Finally, whatever happens, don't let yourself be moved from your negotiating position just because the other side engages in petty or antisocial behavior. This sets a bad precedent, and if you do so you can bet that you will find yourself facing that behavior repeatedly from that point forward.

The End of the Road

There comes a time when the hiring manager can't go any further in meeting your needs. When you hear something like, "Please consider this our final offer," "I just can't go beyond what I've agreed to already," or "I think your expectations are beyond what we can do"—and you get the sense that the hiring manager means it—continued pushing will only lead to alienation and likely to a negative outcome for you. Better to recognize this and end the discussion politely by saying either, "Thank you very much. I appreciate your efforts to meet my needs, and you can be sure I'll do my best to meet your expectations" (if you are accepting the offer), or "Thank you very much. I appreciate your efforts to meet my needs, and I'll give your offer careful thought" (if you're not ready to accept it).

Note: If you do succeed in cutting a special deal that might be the envy of your peers, be discreet about it. You won't score any points by causing unhappiness in your work group and making your manager regret trying to accommodate you.

Advanced Negotiation Techniques

Now that you have a good handle on basic negotiation techniques, we'll look at a few advanced techniques that you should consider adding to your repertoire as you develop your negotiation skills and your comfort with making arguments on the fly.

Avoiding the Faulty Premise

The best debaters, lawyers, and negotiators have one technique they rely on more than any other to win arguments: They state a starting premise (basic facts and assumptions) that serves only their argument, get you to agree to that premise, and then let the discussion follow from there. Guess what: You won't win an argument when the other side has stacked the deck against you with one or more unchallenged faulty premises.

Remember this the next time you find yourself losing an argument that you are confident you should be winning; take a step back and think about the premises you have agreed to along the way. Are those the basic facts and assumptions as you would have characterized them? Do they sound right on their surface, but have some fine nuances that can change their nature and interactions, depending on outside factors or information? Does the premise require you to rely solely on facts and assumptions provided or controlled by the other side—and lacking third-party empirical support?

Consider the following examples of how agreeing to a faulty premise can prevent you from winning your point:

Employer: The salary comparison sources you find online are usually about 6 months behind reality. This industry is shrinking, so of course salaries in this industry are shrinking as well.

Employer: After the technology bust, no one covers 100 percent of health insurance premiums anymore. We offer the next best thing in today's environment, a 50 percent employer contribution.

Employer: Wouldn't you agree that your resume has a marketing focus that could be developed more highly with the right kind of mentorship? Let's start you off as an assistant to one of our marketing associates.

Employer: As you would imagine, junior sales personnel start at a lower commission percentage than senior sales personnel do.

See where the net closes in each example? Don't let yourself get sucked into agreeing to this sort of premise in a negotiation. If you don't have data to confirm or controvert a premise, ask probing questions to tease out the sources for the premise and side-step the premise where you don't feel you are getting the whole story. This may mean that you call out the premise and tell the other side directly that you would like to bypass negotiating the current term until you have had a chance to research the premise.

Finally, don't let your lack of experience with a subject embarrass you into agreeing to a faulty premise; this is a very common mistake that leads people to agree to unfavorable deals all the time. It is much better to either ask for further explanation or ask to shelve that part of the discussion until you have had a chance to better inform yourself.

Here are some suggestions for side-stepping the above premises:

Candidate: The industry may be shrinking, but your comment on shrinking salaries is surprising to hear as I have been looking at the latest jobs, posted as recently as this week, and haven't noticed any salary depression. And, my understanding is that good candidates are even more valuable in today's more competitive market.

Candidate: Interesting . . . my other interviews in this industry haven't exposed that trend. I am also somewhat surprised that this company, which is in construction, and has reported strong, stable year-over-year growth and revenues, identifies itself with the technology bust.

Candidate: Mentoring is extremely important. In fact, in my last position in product development and marketing, I effectively mentored several sales marketing personnel who worked closely with my department to develop sales marketing materials as the product developed. Given that background, I would be excited to be mentored by the VP of Marketing as I worked in the marketing manager position.

Candidate: Hmm. That surprises me as I would assume that you would want your junior salespeople just as hungry to land business as your senior salespeople—and reducing the commission percentage for junior salespeople further weights their overall compensation package toward salary and not commission, which can decrease a salesperson's drive to complete each additional sale.

Note that none of these arguments is a slam-dunk, but each is plausible. Their value is in moving the discussion away from the employer's premise and preventing the hiring manager from locking in assumptions early into the negotiation that could strangle the candidate's final compensation package.

Acknowledging the Dance

You know that you are asking for more than you expect to get in the negotiation and, guess what, the hiring manager probably knows it, too. Conversely, you will often know that the employer's initial offer is just their starting point for negotiation—and the hiring manager may know that you know this.

Is there anything you can do to manipulate this situation? Probably not if you are not a glib speaker, but keep in mind that there are certain situations in which a sharp negotiator can short-circuit a drawn-out negotiation by openly acknowledging that the parties know that the outcome will be a fixed point between the parties' starting positions—and by slyly stating the assumptions that will drive the negotiation in such a way as to hem in the other side and raise the expected outcome. We do not recommend that you try this unless you are skilled at guessing the other side's settlement range and have the verbal skills to offer your assessment of their position without irritating them irrevocably.

While you should probably avoid this end-game technique, it is not uncommon to find yourself on its receiving end. This is often the case when negotiating with a hiring manager who manages dozens of hires a year and has reached the jaded point where the very act of negotiation has become pro forma. Here are some examples and how to deal with them:

Employer: We advertised the position at $50,000. You are looking to make $60,000. Why don't we skip the back-and-forth and split the difference? You will be able to start on Monday, as you were hoping, and we will definitely revisit your compensation level at the next review.

Response 1

Candidate: Before we move to that discussion, could we discuss some additional questions I have about the position's responsibilities?

Does this reply look familiar? It should—it is a return to value-increasing fundamentals.

Response 2

Candidate: Thanks for offering to shorten the negotiation process for me; it is nice to know that you are also excited about my starting as soon as possible. I appreciate the offer but would like to show you some industry salary data that I think directly informs this discussion and will drive my decision to come on board.

Recognize the response based on data? Very effective in this situation.

Bluffing

Whether or not you have the intestinal fortitude to bluff is up to you to decide: We can't advise you to take on more risk than your personality can reasonably handle. If you have a risk-loving personality and you are confident in your ability to land other competing offers in a timely fashion, then you might consider bluffing your position. However, if you really need *this* job and you are risk-averse, follow the techniques outlined in this Insider Guide and defend your asking terms with the rational, data-supported arguments we have provided.

The Decision

- Get the Final Offer in Writing

- Competing Offers: Consult Your Decision Matrix

- Declining Graciously

- Delaying Your Decision

- When to Say Yes

Congratulations! You have made yourself *the* candidate for a position, used the tools you learned in this Insider Guide to negotiate the best terms possible for that position, and now the employer is ready to make you a final offer. You should be very proud of yourself for having successfully navigated the most difficult parts of the hiring process.

That said, you are not done just yet. Before you make any decision on a final offer, you will want to make sure that the offer is in the appropriate form, assess it against your other offers, make your decision on the offer, and then respond to the offer in a professional manner—regardless of what your final decision may be.

Get the Final Offer in Writing

When the time comes, make sure you receive a written final offer that clearly states the following:

- Your title and major responsibilities

- Your start date

- The person to whom you will report

- Your salary

- Other promised forms of compensation, such as bonuses and commissions, and what you have to do to receive them

- Any promised stock options, the dates they will be granted, the strike price, and the vesting schedule

- Perks, such as a moving allowance, tuition reimbursement, extra vacation time, flextime, early salary review, or any other special arrangements you agreed on

The offer should be written on company letterhead and signed by the hiring manager or someone else with the authority to commit the company to the terms described. A verbal offer is subject to erosion by reinterpretation, faulty recollection, the desire of the company to elude any special arrangements you managed to negotiate, or the migration of the hiring manager within the company or to another job. And it's worthless in court. A written offer—really a contract, once you've signed it—protects you from backpedaling. If it seems too difficult for the company to prepare such a letter (executives at start-ups, for example, are often too busy to follow up), you can write it yourself and get a senior executive to sign it. Remember, though, that ambiguous language is interpreted to the disadvantage of the person who drafts the contract. Make sure every point is crystal clear if you are the one who writes the letter.

You may have already received a written offer from the company. If your negotiations have led to only minor changes, you may be able to simply strike out the language as necessary, write in the changes and initial them, have the person who signed the letter initial them, and sign and date the agreement. That said, most companies will prefer to prepare a clean letter with the changes incorporated. Make sure you end up with a signed copy of the final agreement and file it in a safe place.

Competing Offers:
Consult Your Decision Matrix

You've honed your negotiating skills and received a fine offer from Company X. It's decision time. If you've gone this far, this should be a job you want. But is it *the* job? The answer may not be immediately obvious. If you've been promised an offer within days from Company Y—one that rates considerably higher on your decision matrix, you may want to delay. The choice is tougher if you've just learned of an opportunity at Company Y. Delay may cost you the job with Company X, and you may never get an offer from Company Y. Company X's offer also presents a dilemma if you've just begun your job search and have no idea what else may be out there. Maybe a dream job at Company Z will come up, and maybe nothing else will even compare with Company X's offer.

Let's return to your decision-matrix (see the "Obtaining the Offer" chapter): If Company X scores 850 or above, it's probably not a bad offer to accept, unless you are the type who draws on an 18 in blackjack. If Company X scores in the 600s or lower and you're at an early stage of your job campaign, you may want to tell Company X you're not ready to make a decision and let the chips fall where they may. There's a good chance you'll find something better. If you've been looking for a while, this is a tougher call. It's hard to turn down a certain offer on the hope that you'll find something better. And yet, if you've made plenty of contacts and had numerous information meetings, you should eventually come up with an offer that scores above 600. Hold out if you can afford to, perhaps by taking on project work—especially if you can do it at a place you'd like to work on a long-term basis.

If your choice is between two companies rating in the 800s, you may find yourself agonizing over which way to go. Ask a friend to listen to how you describe both opportunities and tell you which you seem to prefer. If that doesn't work, try it with a former co-worker you respect. In the end, you can always flip a coin—you probably won't go wrong with either job. Consider yourself lucky to be able to pick from two appealing offers.

Declining Graciously

When you've negotiated as far as you can and the offer still falls short, it's time to cut bait and fish elsewhere. And when you reach this conclusion, act decisively. You owe it to the company, which has devoted considerable time to interviewing and negotiation with you, to call the manager and relay your decision to pursue other opportunities. You should follow up this call with a letter or e-mail thanking the hiring manager for his time and efforts on your behalf. Graciousness ensures that you will be remembered favorably—you don't want burn any bridges. Failure to promptly notify the company of your decision— or to do so politely—could come back to haunt you later in your career.

Delaying Your Decision

You're waiting for an offer from Company Y and want to hold off on responding to company X. Be reasonable—you can't expect a company to wait a month while you make up your mind. You can usually get a week or 10 days of breathing space, though. If all your negotiations so far have been verbal, ask to receive the terms you've agreed on in writing. It usually takes a few days for everyone involved to sign off on the offer, and you can be "out of town" or otherwise temporarily unavailable when it arrives. Then you can reasonably request a few days to consider the offer, and possibly clarify a few more points. By the time any revisions you agree on are approved and sent back to you again, 10 days will have elapsed. If you've received the offer from Company Y by now, make it clear that you're going to have to turn down another offer. Company Y should then proceed with you promptly and in good faith. If Company Y still has not made an offer, you might give one more notice of your need to make an immediate decision. Company Y will either act quickly to make you an offer, convey regret that it can't act more quickly (so if you turn down Company X, it's at your own risk), or wave you off.

When to Say Yes

Does the final offer meet your expectations and needs? Is it the best one you have gotten and can reasonably hope for? If you don't accept an offer when the time is ripe—when your negotiations have yielded whatever they're going to yield—it may vanish. Once the company concludes that you're impossible to satisfy, it will turn immediately to other options. There's always a backup candidate or a backup plan, and you should keep this in mind before letting a good opportunity pass you by. Especially if a small element of rancor intruded in your final negotiations, now is the time to express your delight at the opportunity to work at such a great company. You want to start your new job with everyone glad to see you, not resentful!

Negotiating Once You Have the Job

- Preparing for Your Next Review

- Negotiation Requirements

- Making Your Case

- When Your Employer Thinks the Grass Is Greener

- Stepping Outside the Review Process

Preparing for Your Next Review

Depending on your performance, your manager's style, and your company's fiscal health and HR philosophy, you may find that securing a raise or rising through the ranks can be a trying experience. Even good companies with good managers experience downward pressures on labor-related expenses that can stymie the kind of financial and professional development you hope for each time you walk into an employee review. And—at their least benign—employers know that the stress and financial cost of finding and moving to another job are high. They correctly assume that inertia will help keep you from finding and leaving for greener pastures.

Here are some ways to prepare for your next review and compensation negotiation:

1. Keep track of your accomplishments—this doesn't need to be much more than a running shorthand list of the significant tasks you have taken on successfully. (Note that this list can also be quickly integrated into your resume when you decide to go on interviews.)

2. Keep your skill set and professional qualifications up to date. Be aggressive about this: Your documented skill set and professional qualifications constitute your passport between jobs—and thus your negotiation leverage against a recalcitrant employer.

3. Update your resume every few months and go on interviews when offered, or when you have a big review coming up. If interviewing would create immediate problems with your employer, test the market informally by talking to potential employers and your peers at places like conferences, conventions, union events, and job fairs.

4. Benchmark, benchmark, benchmark! Regularly research the going rate for your skill set, your industry, and your position. Don't let yourself get caught out when market demand for your skill set goes up but you are late to notice and capitalize on the change.

5. Use your firsthand knowledge of the decision-maker to increase your leverage. This often involves fine-tuning your work performance in the months before a compensation review to the decision-maker's peculiar tastes. For example, the decision-maker has a pet peeve about paperwork being left on employee desks, so you spend extra time ensuring that your desk is immaculate whenever you leave the office.

Negotiation Requirements

Before you enter the room to negotiate your package as an existing employee, you should have the following:

1. Concrete knowledge of the market's valuation of your skill set and your position or title.

2. A firm understanding of how valuable you are to the company (but remember: almost no one is irreplaceable).

3. A sense of how easy it would be for the company to replace you, either by internal promotion or by outside hiring.

4. A prepared presentation outlining each of the following in detail:

   - The importance of the job you do
   - The special talents and skills you bring to the job
   - Your list of accomplishments at the company thus far

5. A willingness and ability to leave and find a new job if you don't get at least your walk-away terms (see the "What's Negotiable" chapter for more information on developing your settlement ranges). This is necessary as you may occasionally encounter a manager who uses your employee review as an opportunity to bid you far below your minimum asking terms—and even below the terms you are currently enjoying in your job. This last situation tends to happen in an environment where the company or department has suffered financial setbacks, or where the employer feels you haven't measured up to initial expectations. As you can imagine, this employer behavior typically comes as an extreme shock to an employee who has walked into the negotiation equipped solely with his list of requested increases. Don't be hasty in threatening to walk away, but also don't be forced into agreeing to go below what you need to live on and what you know you can make elsewhere.

Making Your Case

Once you are in the negotiation meeting, you should attempt to hew to a tight structure to keep the discussion heading in the desired direction. Here is a structure we have used with success in the past:

1. Start by relating how much you like the company, the team, and the decision-maker—and how excited you are about the future of the company and the industry.

2. Articulate your impression of the importance of your job to the company. Where appropriate, discuss the position's impact on key areas like sales, customer satisfaction, product development, time to market, expense and liability reduction, and morale.

3. Remind the manager of the special talents, skills, and professional qualifications you bring to the job.

4. Run through the list of your significant accomplishments at the company thus far. Resist the temptation to be shy, embarrassed, or self-effacing here: This is your one chance to highlight how much you really do for your employer. Where appropriate, discuss your positive personal impact on the key areas discussed in item 2.

5. Briefly describe some challenges facing you, the department, and the company and then talk about how you plan to conquer them efficiently. This presentation should be tight and on-point: A poorly articulated or ill-considered plan can damage your negotiating position severely. If this discussion seems to go over well with the manager, wrap up your discus-

sion of challenges by stating how much you hope to be able to stay on and solve these issues.

This last comment is the first time that you hint that there is any chance of your leaving the company. It is veiled and fairly easy to back away from if the employer gets aggressive about your implication and threatens to take you up on the offer. Defend it politely but with assurance when you are confident in your demands and you don't fear entering the job market; for example: "I would love to stay here, but I am also interviewing elsewhere, and, as you know, it is very important to me to continue forward in my career development." Back off and explain away the comment when you know that you are insecure in your position and leaving is not a realistic option. Explain it away by replying: "I meant I hope that you are also eager to have me stay and take on these challenges."

6. Ask for the manager's thoughts on the appropriate compensation structure for you, given the discussion you have just had.

7. Use the offer-negotiation tactics outlined in "The Negotiation" to increase and finalize the offer.

If you get knocked out of your presentation sequence, don't get flustered. Gently steer the conversation back to your next talking point as soon as the employer finishes her comment or question. Use each of the manager's interjections as an opportunity to not only address the manager's topic, but also as an opening to segue back to your next point. Remember, you should absolutely be solicitous of the manager, but not let yourself be cowed into forgoing a formal opportunity, like an employee review, to put your full case on the table.

When Your Employer Thinks the Grass Is Greener

It is an unfortunate fact of the business world that employers tend to pay new employees coming into a position more than they pay the employees currently working under the same title and responsibilities. You may know the job and fit into the company's systems, needs, and culture better than any new hire, but the employer will often fight your request for more compensation and perks harder than the employer would if it were negotiating an offer for the same job with a qualified applicant off the street. This is simply a case of the grass-is-greener syndrome—employers forget that prospective new employees have buffed their resumes and interview presentations to a blinding high gloss that can seem irresistible. In reality, those new employees may actually be a drain on company time and resources until they get up to speed—and even then, they may never be as good at the job as you are right now.

In such a situation, when you reasonably believe that you are being undercompensated in relation to new hires into positions similar to your own, add the following to your review approach (in addition to the structure outlined above):

1. If you have access to applicant resumes and cover letters for new hires into your department, look through them regularly to see how you stack up against your peers. Note the presentation style, content, and stress—and don't be afraid to co-opt into your review presentations the language and approaches that seem to be working for new hires.

2. In your recitation of your special skills, qualifications, accomplishments, and challenges (items 2–4 in the previous section), take appropriate opportunities to stress your capabilities and advantages over a new hire coming into the position cold.

3. Keep track of new-hire integration issues and expenses. Don't be petty and be careful of criticizing the manager or their favorite employees, but be ready in your negotiation to present an impersonal analysis of the typical effort and expense to bring new personnel into similar positions—and highlighting any associated productivity or revenue dips. Note: You will not want to trot out this analysis unless you just can't get the manager to meet compensation demands in line with those being honored for new employees.

Stepping Outside the
Review Process

Are you doing an amazing job? Are you getting attractive solicitations or offers from other employers? Has a boss or co-worker left your department, leaving you to do that job, as well as your own? If you are substantially exceeding the original terms of your employment, or you are receiving clear signals that the market values you more than your current employer, it is time to schedule a formal meeting with your manager to discuss your request for an accelerated review of your compensation, title, or both—to take place soon.

Once you are in the meeting, you should follow the same general structure you would for a scheduled review, with emphasis on your increased responsibilities or the attractiveness of competing offers.

For Your Reference

- A Primer for First-Time Job-Seekers

- Additional Advice for Midcareer Candidates

- Additional Resources

- About the Authors

A Primer for First-Time Job-Seekers

Is this your first time finding a job that doesn't involve fast food, cutting grass, or babysitting? Do you feel like you are walking to the gallows without knowing what gallows even look like? Quit worrying! Here is a quick general primer on what you can expect when you go for your first real job negotiation, broken down by size of employer.

Large Company Interview and Negotiation Process

You can expect to deal primarily with a human resources manager (or recruiter) who collects resumes, culls them against the reporting manager's instructions and requirements, and sets up initial interviews. Your first interview may be a phone or face-to-face interview with the HR manager or recruiter, who will be vetting you and your resume for honesty, obvious competence, and appropriateness to the position being hired. Once you clear that hurdle, you may be passed to the manager, to whom you would report in the job, for further interviews. And that manager may very well be the decision-maker from whom you will receive the offer—and with whom you will negotiate the offer. If this is the case, just follow the structure outlined in the earlier chapters of this Insider Guide and you will be on track to secure and maximize your offer.

On the other hand, for lower-level positions—particularly in large or administrative departments—the HR manager may be tasked with making your offer and even negotiating it. And while the HR manager may be the person you are forced to negotiate with, you should try everything appropriate to present yourself and your resume directly to the job's reporting manager. The reporting manager may not want or be authorized to negotiate directly with you, but he can be a tremendous ally in convincing the HR manager that you are the candidate that the department must have—which increases your bargaining power.

Negotiating with HR Managers and Recruiters

HR managers and recruiters are generally quite competent, but, given the broad nature of their responsibilities, they may not understand all of the exigencies of a specific job they have been tasked with hiring, nor can they comprehend the full value of unusual skill sets or resumes. So, their tendency is to play the hiring decision safely and go with the obvious candidate who best checks all of the basic boxes and is presentable. Thus, you would be well served to conform your resume closely to the posted job requirements and emphasize your applicable skills in simple, direct language in your cover letter.

Most important, once you get an offer from an HR manager you may find that there is little opportunity for a sophisticated negotiation. You will typically discuss the offer over the telephone, or be asked to come in to meet in the manager's office. The time allotted for the call or meeting will be 30 minutes or less and it is not uncommon to find that the HR manager is only authorized to negotiate salary (and perhaps vacation) terms—and their negotiation range is likely be highly constrained. That said, do not assume severe constraints from the outset: Ask brief but probing questions about the offer to try to discover the set of negotiable items under the HR manager's control.

This constrained situation can be frustrating, but you can still push the negotiable issues with the skills you learned in this Insider Guide. Do so patiently, realizing that you are dealing with someone who may not fully understand the value of the job, let alone the value of *you* doing it. Stick to the basic interview and negotiation approaches you have learned and you should be able to move the HR manager closer to your position on the issues on which she has been authorized to negotiate.

Finally, you should keep in mind that there may be an opportunity to ask the HR manager for an accelerated review schedule. In your first job, a concession giving you an early review can be more important than a concession on any other issue than your starting salary. Therefore, once you have reached the end of the road in your salary (and perhaps vacation) negotiation, consider pushing hard for an accelerated first compensation review, stressing it as the final thing stopping you from accepting the offer immediately—and reinforcing that an early review is important to you because you know that you will knock the ball out of the park in your new job. An HR manager who has gone through the entire interview and negotiation process and senses that he is very close to successfully hiring the position (and thus clearing the task from his in-box), may be willing to use some of his own internal political capital to secure this additional concession for you.

Medium Company Interview and Negotiation Process

Again, you can expect to interact initially with a human resources manager (or outside recruiter) who collects resumes, culls them per the reporting manager's instructions and requirements, and sets up initial interviews. Your first interview may be a phone or face-to-face interview with the HR manager, who will be vetting you and your resume for honesty, obvious competence, and appropriateness to the position being hired. Once you clear that hurdle, you will probably be passed to the manager to whom you would report for further interviews.

When an offer is tendered, it will likely be by the reporting manager and you will then negotiate with them directly. Follow our instructions in the earlier chapters of this Insider Guide to maximize your chances of a great final offer!

Small Company Interview and Negotiation Process

In a start-up or small business, it is common to discover that the job was posted directly by the decision-maker—who may also be the owner or a senior executive. And that hiring manager may personally manage the entire interview, offer presentation, and negotiation process. This can mean a less formalized process at each step and give you a great opportunity to really connect personally with the decision-maker and help her see how important the job is and how valuable you would be in that job. Use the skills we have outlined in this Insider Guide to build your bargaining power and capitalize on the personal connection that you can make in this situation!

Additional Advice for Midcareer Candidates

You've been around the job block a few times and have developed a resume with a clear plot that tells a cogent story about you and your career thus far. You have real references, friendships with peers in your field and industry, and, best of all, you have demonstrable skills and professional credibility. These factors all contribute to increased bargaining power and can leave you feeling more confident as you enter the job search process.

However, you may also feel a degree of trepidation about putting yourself back on the job market, particularly if you have been at the same employer for years and there appear to be lots of seemingly qualified young hotshots competing with you. Don't get psyched out: Stay disciplined in your job search and bone up on the latest interviewing advice, found in the earlier chapters of this Insider Guide and in WetFeet's Insider Guide to interviewing, *Ace Your Interview!*). Remember this: Your experience and maturity will eventually win the day.

In addition to the tips offered in earlier chapters, midcareer candidates should keep the following in mind when interviewing and negotiating for a new position:

1. Your research and benchmarking should be done at least partially through your mentor and peer networks in the profession and industry—some of them hopefully at the target employer. This type of data is particularly useful as it is tightly focused and personally vouched.

2. Prospective employers will tend to be responsive to your attempts to establish personal connections with the hiring manager and departmental team

members while interviewing. Take every opportunity to sink strong personal hooks into the other side; you will be able to push harder and longer in your offer negotiation because of these connections.

3. Depending on your profession and industry, you may very well know how many other candidates you are competing against—and maybe even exactly who those competitors are. This can provide a great opportunity to tune your presentation to highlight your peculiar advantages over those competitors (keep it impersonal: we do not recommend mentioning competitors by name). It can also help you to demand a premium for your skill set, client list, name recognition, and demonstrated industry success.

4. When it is time to discuss terms and negotiate your offer, be prepared for more sophisticated horse-trading than you saw earlier in your career. Expect to explore and negotiate a broad variety of compensation possibilities— and assume that the employer will be prepared to negotiate a personalized set of benefits to attract you. Don't miss an opportunity to identify and negotiate for the additional responsibilities, benefits, and perks that may be readily available to someone at your career stage.

Finally, you can generally expect that each new interview and offer negotiation process will be more personal—and even convivial—the more established you become in your career. This does not mean that the negotiations become easier: As you move up the career ladder, the level of hiring manager and his or her negotiation skills also go up accordingly. Don't mistake greater respect and friend-liness for an unwillingness to negotiate aggressively—skilled negotiators can make you feel completely at home while they grind your position down. Encourage friendly interaction during the negotiation, but stay focused on your negotiation goals and on making the supporting arguments necessary to achieve them.

Additional Resources

Benchmarking Resources

America's Career InfoNet

Find median wages for your chosen field in your geographic location, what it takes for you to get ahead in your occupation, and which careers have the strongest outlook right now: www.acinet.org.

Bureau of Labor Statistics

Search the Career Guide to Industries and the Occupational Outlook Handbook to research opportunities in your field and explore the most promising career options. The Occupational Employment Statistics will help you identify mean salaries, the current rate of layoffs, and wage comparisons for your industry and geographic location: www.bls.gov/oco/home.htm.

Professional Association for Compensation, Benefits, and Total Rewards

Check out the latest research on performance-based pay, stock options, overtime pay, and paid leave though survey briefs and in-depth reports: www.worldatwork.org.

Salary.com

Find appropriate salary and benefits for your position and pick up tips on how to raise your pay, get paid time off, and negotiate cost-of-living increases: www.salary.com.

U.S. Census Bureau

Check out the latest economic census figures as of March 2004, including earnings for your industry, earnings cross-referenced by occupation, education level and gender for your geographic location, and hard numbers on e-commerce: www.census.gov.

Research Tools

Fortune Career Resources

Fortune's annual reports on the best places to work, most admired companies, and the best places to work for women and minorities are key background reading. Also check out their columns to discover jobs you never new existed ("You Do What?"), the latest on workplace practices such as telecommuting and casual dress, and career quizzes: www.fortune.com/fortune/careers.

Business Week Company Research

Get the inside scoop on some 4,000 employers: http://bwnt.businessweek.com:/company/search.asp. While you're there, check out *Business Week*'s "Career Strategies" section for job search strategies for MBAs, downsized midcareer employees, and aspiring executives.

Labor Market Information Center

Find out what occupations are hottest in your geographic area and across the nation: www.careeronestop.org/lmi/LMIHome.asp.

Current Economic Conditions by Federal Reserve District

If you're considering relocating to look for work, use this government index known as the "Beige Book" to identify where the economic prospects are brightest in the United States: www.federalreserve.gov/FOMC/BeigeBook/2004/.

The Conference Board

Concerned about what those economic indicators mean for your industry—and your job prospects? Get expert perspective on business trends using the Conference Board's research: www.conference-board.org.

WetFeet Resources

The following WetFeet titles are all available online at www.WetFeet.com and www.Amazon.com. See the last two pages of this Insider Guide for a complete list of WetFeet Insider Guides.

Ace Your Interview!

Learn what employers are looking for and how to give it to them in an interview, from key preinterview research through interview prep for commonly asked questions and curve balls, through effective follow-up strategies.

Networking Works!

Find out how you can get the jump on those great jobs you hear about but never seem to see postings for, and what it takes to land them yourself, from the initial contact through all-important lunch meetings and follow-up.

Job Hunting A to Z: Landing the Job You Want

This information-packed guide by one of the co-authors of *Negotiating Your Salary and Perks* covers the basics of networking, interviewing, and negotiation all in one handy reference, with tips on drumming up contacts and referrals, handling weird interview situations, and choosing from several offers.

WetFeet's Company Profiles and Interviews

Get the lowdown on hundreds of high-profile employers, including key numbers, personnel highlights, key facts, and an overview for each company. www.wetfeet.com/research/companies.asp.

Additional Reading

Difficult Conversations: How to Discuss What Matters Most

(Douglas Stone, et al. Penguin Putnam, 2000)

A practical guide to the art of handling unpleasant and uncomfortable conversations. Constructive techniques are offered to develop your skills in a variety of situations, along with examples of correct and incorrect approaches.

Getting to Yes: Negotiating Agreement without Giving In

(Roger Fisher and William Ury. Penguin, 1991)

The defining text on principle-driven, problem-solving negotiation techniques. The focus is on negotiation as an attempt to solve both sides' problems, leaving the parties satisfied and willing to meet their obligations under the negotiated agreement.

Getting Past No: Negotiating Your Way from Confrontation to Cooperation

(William Ury, Bantam, 1993)

An extension of *Getting to Yes*, this text concerns itself with getting past negotiation roadblocks, including unethical or unreasonable behavior by the other side.

Telling Lies: Clues to Deceit in the Marketplace, Politics, and Marriage

(Paul Ekman. Norton & Co., 2001)

An outline of the physical cues present when a person is lying, and a guide to reading those cues to detect lying. (Note: This text is dense and, at times, poorly edited, but worth your time if you want to become an expert negotiator.)

The Art of War

(Sunzi [Sun Tzu], translated by Lionel Giles. Dover, 2001)
After getting your fill of the modern, consensus-seeking approaches offered by the preceding texts, it makes sense to cut your palate with a bit of ancient military wisdom. This text is composed solely of simple aphorisms, but these aphorisms are often much pithier and more useful than the most researched of modern approaches. This is a must-read at certain investment houses.

About the Authors

Duncan Haberly, Esq., is a negotiation expert whose specialty is renegotiation and extrication from unworkable or inconvenient commercial deals. Duncan's company, Contracts Inc., provides direct business negotiation services to Silicon Valley companies.

Previously, Duncan headed business development for Military Advantage, Inc. While at Military Advantage, Duncan developed the strategic and content partnerships necessary to launch Military.com, the largest private military-related website on the Internet (subsequently acquired by Monster.com).

Duncan has consulted for a variety of clients, including the Dave Matthews Band's e-commerce and fulfillment division and Apple Computers. Duncan started his legal career as a U.S. Government-sponsored tax law and policy advisor to the Russian Ministry of Finance in Moscow, Russia, and co-authored the joint USAID/IMF Draft Law on Tax Administration submitted to the Russian Duma in 1997. He also managed the effort to develop tax collegia within the Russian Arbitration Court system.

Duncan earned his J.D. at the University of Virginia, where he also received his baccalaureate degrees in German and Russian. Before attending the University of Virginia, Duncan served as an active-duty Russian translator in Army Military Intelligence in Fulda, West Germany, during the last years of the Cold War.

Robert A. Fish, PhD, is an expert on the skills needed to climb the corporate ladder. Over the past 20 years he has personally counseled thousands of executives, managers, and professionals on marketing their talents.

Rob's own career demonstrates his expertise in personal marketing. He founded and heads the consulting firm SageWorks, which provides strategic and marketing advice to companies seeking rapid growth and better bottom lines. Previously, he cofounded Right Management Consultants, Inc., the world's largest outplacement, career-management, and career-transition firm. While there, he developed many of the company's written materials and training programs, and opened offices in several locations.

Earlier, Rob founded and was CEO of a software company that developed decision-analysis products for airlines. And during the Kennedy administration he headed up government studies of major technology issues, such as development of a supersonic transport, satellites for communications and navigation, and remote sensing. He earned his PhD in astrophysics at the University of Chicago and is a graduate of Harvard.

You'll find more of Rob's easy-to-follow, proven strategies in *Job Hunting A to Z: Landing the Job You Want*, an essential tool for networking, interviewing, and landing a job offer.

WETFEET'S INSIDER GUIDE SERIES

JOB SEARCH GUIDES

Getting Your Ideal Internship

Job Hunting A to Z: Landing the Job You Want

Killer Consulting Resumes!

Killer Investment Banking Resumes!

Killer Cover Letters & Resumes!

Negotiating Your Salary & Perks

Networking Works!

INTERVIEW GUIDES

Ace Your Case: Consulting Interviews

Ace Your Case II: 15 More Consulting Cases

Ace Your Case III: Practice Makes Perfect

Ace Your Case IV: The Latest & Greatest

Ace Your Case V: Return to the Case Interview

Ace Your Interview!

Beat the Street: Investment Banking Interviews

Beat the Street II: I-Banking Interview Practice Guide

CAREER & INDUSTRY GUIDES

Careers in Accounting

Careers in Advertising & Public Relations

Careers in Asset Management & Retail Brokerage

Careers in Biotech & Pharmaceuticals

Careers in Brand Management

Careers in Consumer Products

Careers in Entertainment & Sports

Careers in Human Resources

Careers in Information Technology

Careers in Investment Banking

Careers in Management Consulting

Careers in Manufacturing

Careers in Marketing & Market Research

Careers in Nonprofits & Government Agencies

Careers in Real Estate

Careers in Supply Chain Management

Careers in Venture Capital

Consulting for PhDs, Doctors & Lawyers

Industries & Careers for MBAs

Industries & Careers for Undergrads

COMPANY GUIDES

Accenture

Bain & Company

Boston Consulting Group

Booz Allen Hamilton

Citigroup's Corporate & Investment Bank

Credit Suisse First Boston

Deloitte Consulting

Goldman Sachs Group

J.P. Morgan Chase & Company

Lehman Brothers

McKinsey & Company

Merrill Lynch

Morgan Stanley

25 Top Consulting Firms

Top 20 Biotechnology & Pharmaceuticals Firms

Top 25 Financial Services Firms